How

11 MILLION PEOPLE?

Why the Truth Matters More Than You Think

ANDY ANDREWS

W PUBLISHING GROUP

AN IMPRINT OF THOMAS NELSON

Contact Andy
To book Andy for corporate events, call
(800) 726-ANDY (2639).
For more information, go to
www.AndyAndrews.com.

Compilation © 2020 by W Publishing, an imprint of Thomas Nelson.

Part One: *How Do You Kill 11 Million People?* © 2011 by Andy Andrews

Part Two: Compilation of public-domain documents and original content extracted from *The Portable Patriot: Documents, Speeches, and Sermons that Compose the American Soul* © 2010 by Joel J. Miller and Kristen Parrish. Used by permission.

All rights reserved. No portion of this book may be reproduced, stored in a retrieval system, or transmitted in any form or by any means—electronic, mechanical, photocopy, recording, scanning, or other—except for brief quotations in critical reviews or articles, without the prior written permission of the publisher.

Interior illustrations by Wayne Brezinka.

Thomas Nelson titles may be purchased in bulk for educational, business, fund-raising, or sales promotional use. For information, please email SpecialMarkets@ ThomasNelson.com.

Any Internet addresses, phone numbers, or company or product information printed in this book is offered as a resource and are not intended in any way to be or to imply an endorsement by Thomas Nelson, nor does Thomas Nelson vouch for the existence, content, or services of these sites, phone numbers, companies, or products beyond the life of this book.

ISBN 978-0-7852-3457-9 (SC)
ISBN 978-0-7852-3458-6 (eBook)

Printed in the United States of America

21 22 23 24 LSC 10 9 8 7 6 5 4 3

Contents

CONTENTS

Author's Note

For many years I have been asked to speak to political gatherings of one type or another. And for many years I have consistently declined. Because the books I write are generally regarded as commonsense literature—novels that illustrate life's principles—I suppose many politicians have simply assumed that I was on their side. However, I am not an "us or them" kind of person. Actually, I am more of a "we" person.

Don't get me wrong—I do have some absolutes carved into my heart and mind, but I am optimistic enough to believe there is still common ground even with those of us who might disagree. Don't we all want the best for our country and a secure and prosperous future for our children? Of course we do. And I believe that we can talk about divisive subjects without screaming at each other.

Somehow, for the most part, our parents and grandparents managed to disagree with their neighbors and still remain neighborly. And they usually did it from their front porches. Today, most of us don't even have front porches. We have retreated to the backyard, where a single opinion can be isolated and enforced by a privacy fence.

Several years ago I asked myself these three questions: Where do we begin to find common ground in regard to what we want (or don't want) for the future of America? Is it possible to write something that doesn't use the words *Republican* or *Democrat*, *liberal* or *conservative*, yet conveys a message with which everyone could agree? Can it be written in a concise fashion allowing anyone to read it, clearly understand the message, and be empowered in less than fifteen minutes?

In answer to those questions, I wrote the first edition of this book, published in 2011 under the title *How Do You Kill 11 Million People?* It quickly became a *New York Times* bestseller. In the years since then, it has become even more urgent that these questions be addressed. America faces perhaps its greatest crisis, domestically and internationally, since its birth.

People often ask me if I have a political agenda. Of course I do. And I sure hope you have one too. Here's mine: I want America's present and future leadership to embrace and live up to America's core principles as written by our Founding Fathers and set forth in those important documents on which the soul of America was composed.

So, in addition to the text of the first edition of *How Do You Kill 11 Million People?*, you'll find a carefully assembled sampling of American history's most formative words, written by the people who made that extraordinary history. While peering back to the cradle of America's national identity combined with an exploration of a number of issues and questions relevant to our lives today, here is my wake-up call for you to become an informed, passionate citizen who demands honesty and integrity from your leaders. We can no longer measure a leader's worth by the yardsticks provided by the left or the right. Instead, we must use an unchanging standard: the pure, unvarnished truth.

—ANDY ANDREWS
ORANGE BEACH, ALABAMA

The punishment which the wise suffer who refuse to take part in the government, is to live under the government of worse men.[1]

—PLATO

Part One

Truth Matters

1

The Truth Shall Set You Free

For you shall know the truth, and the truth shall set you free."

Those are probably the most famous words ever spoken on the subject of truth. Most of us accept that particular sentence at face value. It certainly resonates with our spirit. It just feels right. But what does it mean, really? And have you ever contemplated the meaning that comes to light by inverting this principle?

If it is correct that "you shall know the truth, and the truth shall set you free," then is it possible that if you *don't* know the truth, its absence can place you in bondage?

As a boy, I quickly learned that if someone found out the truth, I might get in trouble or I wouldn't get chosen or I wouldn't be as well liked. Yet my parents urged me to tell the truth and went so far as to promise I would not be spanked—if I only told the truth.

At Heard Elementary School, I told my fourth-grade classmates that Elvis Presley was my cousin. I suppose it was my way of courting popularity at the time. But Elvis was not my cousin. What I had publicly declared in the cafeteria was not true, and for a time, though it didn't seem possible, I became even less popular.

It was a good lesson and helped me determine that, in the future, I would tell the truth.

Once, when I was fifteen, a man in our neighborhood told me that he would pay me fifty dollars for a particular task of yard work. When I finished, he gave me twenty dollars and said that was the amount upon which we had agreed. It was the first time someone had ever looked me directly in the eye and purposefully told me something that was not true. I took note several years later when he was publicly shamed and financially penalized for another instance—entirely unrelated to me—of not telling the truth.

Through my formative years and on into young adulthood, the truth became a touchstone, a goalpost, something to strive for. The truth was always within my sight, usually respected but sometimes compromised.

Once, I watched on television as the president of the United States resigned his office in disgrace. At that time, it didn't occur to me that the nation was in so much turmoil—and the president was in so much trouble—not because of what had been done, but because he had lied about it.

AS AN ADULT, I have become a student of history. For some reason, I am fascinated by what people said and what nations did so many years ago. I am also interested in results—the outcomes these civilizations produced as they reacted to what people said and what nations did so many years ago.

I often wonder, do those outcomes have any bearing on us today? Should we be more careful students of the events and decisions that have shaped the lives and nations of those who have gone before us?

A long time ago I decided that if history were to be of any value in my life, I could not succumb to the temptation of convenience in regard to my personal beliefs or desires. In other words, I would not be able to categorize people and nations as "good guys" or "bad guys" to suit my political or religious beliefs. The truth in what I uncovered would have to trump everything I had ever been taught or believed. Quietly, I could only hope that what I had been taught and believed was true.

Sometime during my study of the Dark Ages and Middle Ages, I uncovered an odd paradox that exists in our minds about time gone by. It is a difference most people don't discern between history and the past. Simply stated, *the past* is what is real and true, while *history* is merely what someone recorded.

If you don't think there is a difference, experience an event in person and then read about it in the newspaper the next day, after witnesses have been interviewed. It might be shocking for many of us to realize that what we know as "history" can actually be a total fabrication, created from the imagination of someone with an ax to grind. Or perhaps, and it certainly happened in the Middle Ages, history was simply recorded by the man with the sharpest ax.

ON INTO WORLD conquest I read, now aware that to be assured of accurate information it would be vitally important that I confirm records and stories with transcripts and eyewitness accounts where possible.

The records surrounding the life of Joan of Arc—her triumphs, capture, fourteen-month trial, execution, retrial of nullification twenty years after her death, and subsequent canonization—particularly fascinated me. Hundreds of eyewitnesses testified over a period of almost thirty years as to what they personally saw or did not see.

Do we know the truth about the life and death of Joan of Arc today? One would hope so. She is the patron saint of soldiers, martyrs, prisoners, and the entire nation of France.

World history, for those who continue to study

it, becomes more defined during the seventeenth and eighteenth centuries, particularly during the American Revolution. Records by opposing forces and differing beliefs remain in relatively good shape and can still be examined by those wishing to do so.

The people of our present world retain a general awareness of historical time lines and a few specific dramatic events that shaped our lives. We occasionally read history or watch history presented on film. But in terms of why we do what we do, how we govern each other, what our society allows and why—very few of us intentionally connect the truth of the past with the realities of where we have ended up today.

So is the truth of the past even important? What about the truth itself? Beyond the elusive moral ideal by which most of us were raised—being honest and doing good—does the truth really, really matter?

To answer that question
effectively, I would ask
you another question . . .

How do you kill
eleven million
people?

OBVIOUSLY, MOST OF us have never even considered such a thing. Yet when I began to closely research our world's recent history—the last one hundred years—that particular question made its unsettling way into my mind.

How do you kill eleven million people?

Eleven million. The number is so large when the word *people* is attached to it that it becomes almost impossible to take seriously.

"Why eleven million?" you might ask. "What is the significance of that number?"

It is true: there is no *singular* significance in that number. And the actual number is 11,283,000—the number of people recorded who were killed by Adolf Hitler between the years 1933 and 1945.[2] Incidentally, that particular figure only represents institutionalized killing. It does *not* include the 5,200,000 German civilians and military war dead.[3] Neither does it include the 28,736,000 Europeans killed during World War II as a result of Hitler's aggressive governmental policies.[4]

Within the same parameters, we could have used the number of Cambodians put to death by their own government: slightly more than three million between the years 1975 and 1979. Three million—from a total population of eight million.[5]

We could have used the exact figure of 61,911,000. That is the number of people who were murdered by the government of the Soviet Union, shown by their own records, between the years 1917 and 1987. But only 54,767,000 of the men, women, and children put to death by the Communist Party were officially Soviet citizens. That is 14,322 human lives for every word in Part One of this book.[6]

During World War I, the highest leadership council of Turkey's Young Turk government decided to exterminate every Armenian in the country, whether a soldier already on the front lines fighting for the government or a pregnant woman. This government institutionally killed their own famous scholars, their own religious leaders, their own children, and ardent patriots of their own country. All two million of them.[7] We could have used that number instead.

In fact, during our world's last one hundred years, there are many different figures from which to choose. Three million in North Korea.[8] More than a million each in Mexico,[9] Pakistan,[10] and the Baltic States.[11] The choices available, and numbers of dead killed at the hands of their own governments, are staggering. And in other places around the world, they are just getting started.

But for our purpose, let's focus on the number that is probably the most well known to us—the eleven million human beings exterminated by the Nazi regime.

There are many lessons we have learned from that tragic period in history, but one particular part of the story remains quietly hidden from even the most brilliant of scholars. It is the answer to one simple question.

How do
you kill
eleven million
people?

ONLY A CLEAR understanding of the answer to this question and the awareness of an involved populace can prevent history from continuing to repeat itself as it already has, time and again.

To be absolutely clear, the *method* a government employs in order to do the actual killing is not in question. We already know the variety of tools used to accomplish mass murder.

Neither do we need to consider the mind-set of those deranged enough to conceive and carry out a slaughter of innocents. History has provided ample documentation of the damage done to societies by megalomaniacal psychopaths or sociopaths.

What we need to understand is how eleven million people allow themselves to be killed.

Obviously, that is an oversimplification, but think with me here . . . If a single terrorist begins to shoot automatic weapons in a movie theater containing three hundred people, the lone gunman couldn't possibly kill all three hundred. Why? Because when the shooting started, most of the crowd would run. Or hide. Or fight . . .

So why, for month after month and year after year, did millions of intelligent human beings—guarded by a relatively few Nazi soldiers—willingly load their families into tens of thousands of cattle cars to be transported by rail to one of the many death camps scattered across Europe? How can a condemned group of people headed for a gas chamber be compelled to act in a docile manner?

The answer is breathtakingly simple. And it is a method still being used by some elected leaders to achieve various goals today.

How do you kill eleven million people?

Lie to them.

ACCORDING TO TESTIMONY provided under oath by witnesses at the Nuremberg Trials (including specific declarations made in court on January 3, 1946, by former SS officers), the act of transporting the Jews to death camps posed a particular challenge for the man who had been named operational manager of the Nazi genocide. Adolf Eichmann, known as "The Master," was directed by written order in December 1941 to implement the Final Solution.

Eichmann went about the task as if he were the president of a multinational corporation. He set ambitious goals, recruited enthusiastic staff, and monitored the progress. He charted what worked and what didn't and changed policy accordingly. Eichmann measured achievement in quotas filled. Success was rewarded. Failure was punished.

An intricate web of lies, to be delivered in stages, was designed to ensure the cooperation of the condemned (but unknowing) Jews. First, as barbed-wire fences were erected, encircling entire neighborhoods, Eichmann or his representatives met with Jewish leaders to assure them that the physical restrictions being placed upon their community (in what later became known as ghettos) were only temporary necessities of war. As long as they cooperated, he told them, no harm would come to those inside the fence.

Second, bribes were taken from the Jews in the promise of better living conditions. The bribes convinced the Jews that the situation was indeed temporary and that no further harm would befall them. *After all*, they reasoned, *why would the Nazis accept bribes if they only intend to kill us and take everything anyway?* These first two stages of deception were conducted to prevent uprisings or even escape.

Finally, Eichmann would appear before a gathering of the entire ghetto. Accompanied by an entourage of no more than thirty local men and officers of his own—many unarmed—he addressed the crowd in a strong, clear voice. According to sworn statements, these were very likely his exact words:

> Jews: At last, it can be reported to you that the Russians are advancing on our eastern front. I apologize for the hasty way we brought you into our protection. Unfortunately, there was little time to explain. You have nothing to worry about. We want only the best for you. You will leave here shortly and be sent to very fine places

indeed. You will work there, your wives will stay at home, and your children will go to school. You will have wonderful lives. We will all be terribly crowded on the trains, but the journey is short. Men? Please keep your families together and board the railcars in an orderly manner. Quickly now, my friends, we must hurry![12]

The Jewish husbands and fathers were relieved by the explanation and comforted by the fact that there weren't more armed soldiers. They helped their families into the railcars. The containers, designed to transport eight cows, were each packed with a minimum of one hundred human beings and quickly padlocked.

At that moment they were lost. The trains rarely stopped until well inside the gates of Auschwitz.

Or Belzec.

Or Sobibor.

Or Treblinka . . .

A list drawn up by the German Ministry in 1967 names more than 1,100 concentration camps and subcamps accessible by rail.[13] The Jewish Virtual Library says, "It is estimated that the Nazis established 15,000 camps in the occupied countries."[14]

And **that** is how
you kill eleven million
people.

Lie to them.

But wait, you say.

This didn't happen overnight!

How did things get so

out of hand? How did it

get to this point?

THE NATIONAL SOCIALIST German Workers' Party, led by Adolf Hitler, rose to power during a time of economic uncertainty in a nation of people longing for better times. Germany was a modern, industrialized nation whose well-informed citizens enjoyed ready access to information by way of print and radio broadcast media.

Hitler was a man of the common people—not long before, he had been a lance corporal in the army—and his speeches were exciting and passionate. He promised more and better and new and different. He vowed rapid change and swift action.

According to record, what Hitler actually said in his speeches depended very much upon the audience. In agricultural areas, he pledged tax cuts for farmers and new laws to protect food prices. In working-class neighborhoods, he talked about redistribution of wealth and attacked the high profits generated by business owners. When he appeared before financiers or captains of industry, Hitler focused on his plans to destroy communism and reduce the power of the trade unions.

"How fortunate for leaders," Hitler said to his inner circle, "that men do not think. Make the lie big, make it simple, keep saying it, and eventually they will believe it."[15]

In *Mein Kampf*, Hitler's autobiography, he wrote, "The great masses of the people will more easily fall victim to a big lie than a small one."[16] The book was widely read by the German people at the time.

The masses believed him anyway.

Or at the very most, they ignored him. It is a fact that fewer than 10 percent of Germany's population of 79.7 million people actively worked or campaigned to bring about Hitler's change.[17] Even at the height of its power in 1945, the Nazi political party boasted only 8.5 million members.[18]

So the remaining 90 percent of Germans—teachers and doctors and ministers and farmers—did . . . what? Stood by? Watched?

Essentially, yes.

Mothers and fathers held their voices, covered their eyes, and closed their ears. The vast majority of an educated population accepted their salaries and avoided the uncomfortable truth that lingered over them like a serpent waiting to strike. And when the Nazis came for their children, it was too late.

YOU SEE, IT wasn't only the Jews who were per-secuted. Today, most people are unaware that of the eleven million people exterminated, five million were not even Jewish. In Dachau, one of the largest and most infamous of all concentra-tion camps, only a third of the population was Jewish.

We've all heard of the yellow triangles the Jews were forced to wear for identification. Do you know the other colors that were used?

Brown triangles identified gypsies and those of Roman descent. Purple triangles were worn by Jehovah's Witnesses, Catholic priests, and Christian leaders who ran afoul of the government.

Black triangles marked one as a vagrant—worn by any person lacking documentation when asked for proof of a permanent address. Blue triangles were forced on those who had moved to Germany from other countries, unless they were Jewish, in which case they wore yellow.

Red triangles were worn by a large and diverse group. You wore red if you were a member of a trade union, a Democrat, a Freemason, or any number of categories labeled as a "political non-conformist." Pink badges identified homosexuals, though any suspected perpetrator of a sexual offense such as rape or pedophilia was also given a pink triangle.

Green badges were given to common thieves and murderers. And since they were not suspect politically, these prisoners—called *kapos*—were often in charge of the others.

Purple badges. Red and pink and brown. Blue and black. All worn by mothers and fathers and children who were not the first to be selected for the camps. Their badges were worn—their fates altered—well after they got a good look at the yellow ones.

IN AT LEAST one German town the railroad tracks ran behind the church. An eyewitness stated:

> We heard stories of what was happening to the Jews, but we tried to distance ourselves from it, because we felt, what could anyone do to stop it?
>
> Each Sunday morning, we would hear the train whistle blowing in the distance, then the wheels coming over the tracks. We became disturbed when we heard cries coming from the train as it passed by. We realized that it was carrying Jews like cattle in the cars!
>
> Week after week the whistle would blow. We dreaded to hear the sounds of those wheels because we knew that we would hear the cries of the Jews en route to a death camp. Their screams tormented us.

We knew the time the train was coming and when we heard the whistle blow we began singing hymns. By the time the train came past our church, we were singing at the top of our voices. If we heard the screams, we sang more loudly and soon we heard them no more.

Years have passed and no one talks about it now, but I still hear that train whistle in my sleep.[19]

WITH ALL WE now know, does anyone believe that telling the truth will solve all a nation's problems? Of course not. But it *is* a beginning. In fact, speaking truth should be the *least* we require of our elected leaders! After all, what are *our* standards for being led?

You see, the danger to America is not a single politician with ill intent. Or even a group of them. The most dangerous thing any nation faces is a citizenry capable of trusting a liar to lead them.

In the long run, it is much easier to undo the policies of crooked leadership than to restore common sense and wisdom to a deceived population willing to elect such a leader in the first place. Any country can survive having chosen a fool as their leader. But history has shown time and again that a *nation of fools* is surely doomed.

INCREDIBLY, THERE ARE currently 545 human beings who are directly, legally, morally, and individually responsible for every problem America faces.

Have you ever wondered why America doesn't have a balanced budget? Have you ever in your life heard of a politician who wasn't *for* a balanced budget?

Have you ever heard a politician speak in favor of a complicated tax code that ordinary citizens would find difficult to understand? Then why do we have a complicated tax code that ordinary citizens find difficult to understand?

Meet the 545 men and women who enact every law, propose every budget, and set every policy enforced on the citizens of the United States of America: one president, nine Supreme Court justices, one hundred senators, and 435 members of the House of Representatives.

By the way, have you ever noticed that if any one of us lies to them, it is a felony? But if any one of them lies to us, it is considered politics.

According to the United States Bureau of the Census, our population has now increased beyond 330 million people.[20]

To be clear, that's 545 of them and 330 million of us.

Can 330 million Americans ever hope to wrestle the power away from 545?

One would think so. But did you know that during the past quarter century, no presidential election has been won by more than ten million ballots cast? Yet every federal election during the same time period had at least one hundred million people of voting age who did not bother to vote!

KNOWING THAT THE quality of one's answers can only be determined by the quality of one's questions, let's ask some good ones . . .

Why do the ages of our world's greatest civilizations average around two hundred years?

Why do these civilizations all seem to follow the same identifiable sequence—from bondage to spiritual faith, from spiritual faith to courage, from courage to liberty, from liberty to abundance, from abundance to complacency, from complacency to apathy, from apathy to dependence, and finally from dependence back into bondage?[21]

Is lying to get elected acceptable? Even if the candidate's intention is to get elected in order to do good works?

Is there really any power in one's intentions anyway?

Have you ever noticed how we judge the "bad guys" by their actions and the "good guys" by their intentions?

Who are the good guys and who are the bad guys?

Would truth be a starting point for telling the difference?

What is our nation's course? Do you believe that one can determine a probable destination by examining the direction in which one is traveling? If so, where are we headed?

Can you hear the whistle and the wheels as the train comes down the track?

How
loudly are
you singing?

2

A Conversation with Andy Andrews

1. What are you trying to illustrate with this book?

Other than the subtitle, which is, "Why the truth matters more than you think," what this book illustrates is known as the Principle of the Path, which was first voiced by Andy Stanley. This principle states, "It is direction, not intention, that determines destination."[22] The Principle of the

Path was also discussed in my book *The Traveler's Summit*, a story about what happens when historical figures like Winston Churchill, George Washington Carver, Joan of Arc, and others gather in order to solve a particular challenge. In *The Traveler's Summit* the characters inadvertantly show that history itself is a path that can be examined at any point along the way in order to predict future results.[23]

Similarly, history is merely a broad version of our individual lives: Do we see a pattern in our good choices? Do these good choices lead to good results? Of course they do; therefore, let us continue to make choices just like those good ones that proved beneficial to our lives.

On the other hand, do we see a pattern in some bad choices we have made? Did those bad choices seem to connect the miserable dots that sank our life's results ever lower? Of course they did; therefore, let us determine that we will never make those choices again.

The only way we have to know a person who aspires to lead us is to listen to what he says and watch what he does. Frankly, what *I* might think of any current or past leader of the United States should be irrelevant to you. The questions most important in your life in regard to this subject should be: What criteria do you use to determine who leads your family? And what do *you* think?

2. Are you a Republican or a Democrat?

As I stated in the author's note, I am not an "us or them" kind of person. I am a "we" kind of person. I am a concerned American citizen who demands integrity from those who seek to lead our country. Frankly, I believe candidates from both parties have lied to the American people. Furthermore, I believe that many are slipping dangerously close to creating a habit of lying and rationalizing that their purpose in doing so is "for our own good."

I don't want discussion of this book to devolve into partisan bickering. I did not write this book in order to compare Hitler or the Nazis to any of our current or previous leadership, Republican or Democrat. It might be interesting for the reader to know that the phrase "redistribution of wealth" was not used in the body of this text in order to draw comparisons between Adolf Hitler and any specific person. Actually, I tried to find another way to phrase the point, but ultimately because it illustrated the Führer's style of saying what an audience wanted to hear—and because those particular words actually came from Hitler's mouth—I opted to go with what he really said.

It has become standard operating procedure for many politicians to say whatever is needed in order to get elected. This must stop. History's list is deep and wide and filled with the names of tragic governments whose citizens did *not* stop it.

3. Do you think the German population that allowed Hitler to lead them was a "nation of fools"?

Not necessarily. Germany, at that time, did not have the benefit of examining the history of the kind of tragedies of which they subsequently became a part. They were certainly a nation of misled people. They assumed that the leaders in whom they had placed their faith would put their best interests at the forefront. They were sincere in those beliefs. But as we know now, they were sincerely wrong.

4. Are the American people fools?

I think the jury is still out on that question. I have always considered the American people smart and industrious. Unfortunately, we have all known smart people who have done foolish things. As a group, when more than one hundred million of us don't bother to vote in a federal election, it certainly underscores the "apathy" portion of a nation's fatal sequence.

So are we too trusting? Probably. Are we downright gullible? I'm afraid evidence might support that assertion. But are we fools? I'll give it a "not yet."

5. Are you saying the United States will be the site of the world's next holocaust?

No, I'm not saying that it *will* happen. I am saying that it *could* happen. That's the whole point of the book. History shows that any people who are sheeplike in following their leadership (so long as their personal self-interests are satisfied) may one day awaken to find that their nation has changed in dramatic ways.

It doesn't take many people to lead a nation in a direction that has serious repercussions on the liberty of others. Indeed, most will agree that we have already given up liberties for various reasons, and we may never get them back. Under certain circumstances, things can take a very bad turn very rapidly. This cycle has repeated itself with many societies throughout history. Despite the solid foundation of our culture and political system, America is not immune. As philosopher George Santayana said, "Those who cannot remember the past are condemned to repeat it."[24]

We the people, however, can change this direction. But know this: our portion of history is being written today. What will be remembered about your contribution?

6. Who is lying to our country right now?

Sorry, but I'm simply not going to answer this question. The purpose of this book is to get *you* to answer that question for yourself!

My point is that each of us must stop blindly believing everything someone with an agenda says. Today, with the advent of the Internet's search engines and sites like YouTube, it is fairly simple to verify a politician's promises, voting record, personal life, and so on. So let's all work together. Post your proof online for all of us to read and pass along.

7. Why did you choose to write this book now?

Our nation is at a tipping point. Regardless of political views, people everywhere can sense it. Did you know that the United States of America is now the longest tenured government in the world? There are countries older than us, but as far as one continuous form of government, we are the oldest. Or the last, depending upon how you look at it.

If we don't demand honesty and integrity from America's leadership now—and reward that integrity with our votes—our leaders will lack the fortitude to make the hard decisions that must be made to change course.

If indeed our nation is in a state of crisis, then we need to change before it is too late to choose the direction of that change. We need the correct, and best possible, people in office to make this happen. Some of them, of course, are already in office, but they need our help to surround them with men and women who will do what they believe is right and true.

I wrote this book for you to use as a tool. I wrote it for you to give away. I wrote it for you to discuss and preach about and read to your children. I believe that now, more than ever, America needs to be challenged and inspired to participate.

8. Obviously, there has been public debate and commentary from time to time about one situation or another, but have the American people ever been specifically cautioned about the long-term consequences of electing leaders who lack strong character?

Yes. Few remember the instance, but in retrospect, it is chilling to note the accuracy with which it was delivered. On the occasion of our nation's one hundredth birthday, in his centennial address to Congress in 1876, President James A. Garfield issued a warning widely reported in the press at that time. He said, "Now, more than ever before, the people are responsible for the character of their Congress. If that body be ignorant, reckless, and corrupt, it is because the people tolerate ignorance, recklessness, and corruption. If it be intelligent, brave, and pure, it is because the people demand these high qualities to represent them in the national legislature." Then he added, "If [one hundred years from now] the next centennial does not find us a great nation . . . it will be because those who represent the enterprise, the culture, and the morality of the nation do not aid in controlling the political forces."[25]

9. How can we tell if a politician is telling the truth? Is there a way to know for sure?

You may remember the old joke: "How do you know if a politician is lying? If he's moving his lips." It's not that funny anymore, is it? Obviously, there is no certain way to know at the moment something is said. But remember this: past performance serves to reveal future behavior. A person who has exhibited a pattern of lying is a liar. I know that sounds rough, but can you think of another way to put it? This is why character in our leadership is so important.

In my book *The Traveler's Summit*, Abraham Lincoln says to Joan of Arc, "Does adversity build character? . . . It does not. Almost all people can stand adversity of one sort or another. If you want to test a person's character, give him power."

Continuing, Lincoln says, "Now, since we are concerning ourselves here with the very future of humanity, let me add one thing more. Power corrupts. Trust me on this. And because power corrupts, humanity's need for those in power to be of high character increases as the importance of the position of leadership increases.

"We are discussing character, correct? Not intelligence. Some of the most intelligent leaders in history have brought disaster to their nations because intelligence is powerless to modify character. Great leadership is a product of great character. And this is why character matters."[26]

10. Who should we be listening to?

We should listen to ourselves, listen to common sense, and be mindful of—then heed—what we already know to be true. And we desperately need to be honest with ourselves! We must recognize that, as voters, we sometimes accept a lie when it suits our own self-interest. That's why polls sometimes show that Americans are in favor of throwing everyone out of Congress except *their* representative (at least among those knowing who their representative is).

Obviously, I cannot be in favor of cutting spending and entitlements *except* the ones that benefit me, or my district, or the place where I work. Unfortunately, that's often why we accept lies from politicians. It has become an accepted political strategy for politicians to tell voters the lies we *want* to hear. We, in turn, reward them with elected positions even when we know we're not being told the truth.

11. Why should we believe you're telling the truth?

The Internet can be a wonderful thing. I encourage readers to fact-check what I say in my book against multiple credible sources. That's why I included a bibliography. Read the books yourself . . . examine the record . . . it's all there for anyone to see. And might I add, that's exactly what we should do each time some politician or member of the media says something that doesn't ring true. If we really care to check things out, the lies aren't hard to detect.

12. Do you have a political agenda?

Of course. And I sure hope you have one too. Here's mine: I want America's present and future leadership to embrace and live up to America's core principles as written by our Founding Fathers and set forth in our Constitution. In addition, I want the public to vigilantly hold them accountable for doing so. That is my political agenda.

13. Can you provide an example of a situation in our country that disingenuous leadership is enabling right now?

Certainly. There are many, but one such example was touched on briefly in the body of this work when I wrote, "Have you ever heard a politician speak in favor of a complicated tax code that ordinary citizens would find difficult to understand? Then why do we have a complicated tax code that ordinary citizens find difficult to understand?"

Look, I'm not the smartest guy in the world, but neither am I incredibly stupid. I believe that most folks like me find the days and weeks leading up to April 15 to be—how should I put this?— stressful. Not because we object to paying taxes, but because we fear doing it incorrectly and having to deal with the IRS if we have done so!

The US tax code is so convoluted and bewildering that few of us completely understand it. Yet many politicians actually derive power from it. Through the years, congressional representatives and senators have manipulated the tax code for myriad reasons, such as accepting donations or helping powerful members of their districts back home. In any case, a complex tax code provides a certain cover for shady wheeling and dealing at election time; therefore, there is not much incentive for politicians to simplify the process.

14. Who would you elect president?

Abraham Lincoln, but he won't run again. Beyond that, I am searching for that one special leader who can look us in the eye while telling us the painful truth in such a way that still manages to resonate with voters. That's a tough order, I know, but it can be done. Especially if smart people will get involved in the election process and actually vote.

Part Two

Foundational Truths

1

John Cotton on the Abuse of Power

*John Cotton (1584–1652) was a Puritan
leader who fled to New England in 1633.
A well-respected theologian and preacher, he
became a vital teacher in the Boston church.
Here he wrote on the limitation of government.
Going beyond the bounds God has set, said
Cotton, is both injurious to the people and the
leaders who expand the power given to them.*

L et all the world learn to give mortal men no greater power than they are content they shall use—for use it they will. And unless they be better taught of God, they will use it ever and anon. . . .

It is therefore most wholesome for magistrates and officers in church and commonwealth never to affect more liberty and authority than will do them good, and the people good: for whatever transcendent power is given will certainly overrun those that give it and those that receive it. There is a strain in a man's heart that will sometime or other run out to excess, unless the Lord restrain it; but it is not good to venture it.

It is necessary, therefore, that all power that is on earth be limited, church-power or other. If there be power given to speak great things, then look for great blasphemies, look for a licentious abuse of it. . . .

It is therefore fit for every man to be studious of the bounds which the Lord hath set: and for the people, in whom fundamentally all power lies, to give as much power as God in His word gives to men. And it is meet that magistrates in the commonwealth, and so officers in churches, should desire to know the utmost bounds of their own power, and it is safe for both. All intrenchment upon the bounds which God hath not given, they are not enlargements, but burdens and snares; they will certainly lead the spirit of a man out of his way, sooner or later.

Perry Miller, ed., "Limitation of Government," in *The American Puritans: Their Prose and Poetry* (New York: Columbia University Press, 1982).

2

———

George Washington
on the Question
of Rebellion

*From a July 4, 1774, letter to Bryan
Fairfax contemplating revolution and
the proper response to the ongoing
abuses of the imperial government.*

———

John has just delivered to me your favor of yesterday, which I shall be obliged to answer in a more concise manner, than I could wish, as I am very much engaged in raising one of the additions to my house, which I think (perhaps it is fancy) goes on better whilst I am present, than in my absence from the workmen. . . .

As to your political sentiments, I would heartily join you in them, so far as relates to a humble and dutiful petition to the throne, provided there was the most distant hope of success. But have we not tried this already? Have we not addressed the Lords, and remonstrated to the Commons? And to what end? Did they deign to look at our petitions? Does it not appear, as clear as the sun in its meridian brightness, that there is a regular, systematic plan formed to fix the right and practice of taxation upon us? Does not the uniform conduct of Parliament for some years past confirm this? Do not all the debates, especially those just brought to us, in the House of Commons on the side of government, expressly declare that America must be taxed in aid of the British funds, and that she has no longer resources within herself? Is there any thing to be expected from petitioning after this? Is not the attack upon the liberty and property of the people of Boston, before restitution of the loss to the India Company was demanded, a plain and self-evident proof of what they are aiming at. Do not the subsequent bills (now I dare say acts), for depriving the Massachusetts Bay of its charter, and for transporting offenders into other colonies or to Great Britain for trial, where it is impossible from the nature of the thing that justice can be obtained, convince us that the administration is determined to stick at nothing to carry its point. Ought we not, then, to put our virtue and fortitude to the severest test?

With you I think it a folly to attempt more than we can execute, as that will not only bring disgrace upon us, but weaken our cause; yet I think we may do more than is generally believed, in respect to the non-importation scheme. As to the withholding of our remittances, that is another point, in which I own I have my doubts on several accounts, but principally on that of justice; for I think, whilst we are accusing others of injustice, we should be just ourselves; and how this can be, whilst we owe a considerable debt, and refuse payment of it to Great Britain, is to me inconceivable. Nothing but the last extremity, I think, can justify it. Whether this is now come, is the question. . . .

Jared Sparks, ed., *The Writings of George Washington*, vol. 2 (Boston: Little, Brown, 1855).

3

John Dickinson and Thomas Jefferson on the Causes and Necessity of Taking Up Arms, July 6, 1775

*In April of 1775, the "shot heard round the
world" was fired in Lexington, Massachusetts,
thereby beginning the American Revolution.
On June 14, 1775, the Second Continental
Congress met to adopt the New England
army as its own. It also began assembling
this Declaration, largely the writing of
Thomas Jefferson and John Dickinson, to
substantiate the fighting yet to come.*

We are reduced to the alternative of choosing an unconditional submission to the tyranny of irritated ministers, or resistance by force.—The latter is our choice.—We have counted the cost of this contest, and find nothing so dreadful as voluntary slavery.—Honor, justice, and humanity, forbid us tamely to surrender that freedom which we received from our gallant ancestors, and which our innocent posterity have a right to receive from us. We cannot endure the infamy and guilt of resigning succeeding generations to that wretchedness which inevitably awaits them, if we basely entail hereditary bondage upon them.

Our cause is just. *Our Union is perfect.* Our internal resources are great, and if necessary, foreign assistance is undoubtedly attainable.—We gratefully acknowledge as signal instances of the Divine favor towards us, that his Providence would not permit us to be called into this severe controversy, until we were grown up to our present strength, had been previously exercised in warlike operations, and possessed of the means of defending ourselves. With hearts fortified with these animating reflections, we most solemnly, before God and the world, *declare*, that, exerting the utmost energy of those powers, which our beneficent Creator hath graciously bestowed upon us, the arms we have been compelled by our enemies to assume, we will, in defiance of every hazard, with unabating firmness and perseverance, employ for the preservation of our liberties; *being with one mind resolved to die freemen rather than to live slaves.*

Lest this declaration should disquiet the minds of our friends and fellow subjects in any part of the empire, we assure them that we mean not to dissolve that union which has so long and so happily subsisted between us, and which we sincerely wish to see restored.—Necessity has not yet driven us into that desperate measure, or induced us to excite any other nation to war against them. We have not raised armies with ambitious designs of separating from

Great Britain, and establishing independent States. We fight not for glory or for conquest. We exhibit to mankind the remarkable spectacle of a people attacked by unprovoked armies, without any imputation, or even suspicion of offence. They boast of their privileges and civilization, and yet proffer no milder conditions than servitude or death.

In our own native land, in defence of the freedom that is our birthright, and which we ever enjoyed till the late violation of it—for the protection of our property, acquired solely by the honest industry of our forefathers and ourselves, against violence actually offered, we have taken up arms. We shall lay them down when hostilities shall cease on the part of the aggressors, and all danger of their being renewed shall be removed, and not before.

With an humble confidence in the mercies of

the supreme and impartial Judge and Ruler of the Universe, we most devoutly implore his Divine goodness to protect us happily through this great conflict, to dispose our adversaries to reconciliation on reasonable terms, and thereby to relieve the empire from the calamities of civil war.

Thaddeus Allen, *An Inquiry into the Views, Services, Principles and Influences of the Leading Men in the Origination of Our Union and the Formation and Administration of our Early Government*, vol. 1 (Boston: Saxton & Kelt, 1847).

4

John Adams's Letter to William Cushing (June 9, 1776)

During the momentous days leading up to the Declaration of Independence, John Adams wrote a letter to his friend about "a revolution, the most remarkable, of any."

It would give me great pleasure to ride this eastern circuit with you, and prate before you at the bar, as I used to do. But I am destined to another fate, to drudgery of the most wasting, exhausting, consuming kind, that I ever went through in my whole life. Objects of the most stupendous magnitude, and measures in which the lives and liberties of millions yet unborn are intimately interested, are now before us. We are in the very midst of a revolution, the most complete, unexpected, and remarkable, of any in the history of nations. A few important subjects must be despatched before I can return to my family. Every colony must be induced to institute a perfect government. All the colonies must confederate together in some solemn band of union. The Congress must declare the colonies free and independent States, and ambassadors must be sent abroad to foreign courts, to solicit their acknowledgment of us, as sovereign States, and to form with them, at least with some of them, commercial treaties of friendship and alliance. When these things are once completed, I shall think that I have answered the end of my creation, and sing my *nunc dimittis*, return to my farm, family, ride circuits, plead law, or judge causes, just which you please.

Charles Francis Adams, ed., *The Works of John Adams*, vol. 9 (Boston: Little, Brown, 1854).

5

The Times That Try Men's Souls

From The American Crisis, *by*
Thomas Paine, 1776.

These are the times that try men's souls. The summer soldier and the sunshine patriot will, in this crisis, shrink from the service of their country; but he that stands it now, deserves the love and thanks of man and woman. Tyranny, like hell, is not easily conquered; yet we have this consolation with us, that the harder the conflict, the more glorious the triumph. What we obtain too cheap, we esteem too lightly: it is dearness only that gives every thing its value. Heaven knows how to put a proper price upon its goods; and it would be strange indeed if so celestial an article as FREEDOM should not be highly rated. Britain, with an army to enforce her tyranny, has declared that she has a right (*not only to* TAX) but "to BIND *us in* ALL CASES WHATSOEVER," and if being *bound in that manner*, is not slavery, then there is not such a thing as slavery upon earth. Even the expression is impious; for so unlimited a power can belong only to God.

Whether the independence of the continent was declared too soon, or delayed too long, I will not now enter into as an argument; my own simple opinion is, that had it been eight months earlier, it would have been much better. We did not make a proper use of last winter, neither could we, while we were in a dependent state. However, the fault, if it were one, was all our own;* we have none to blame but ourselves. But no great deal is lost yet. All that Howe has been doing for this month past, is rather a ravage than a conquest, which the spirit of the Jerseys, a year ago, would have quickly repulsed, and which time and a little resolution will soon recover.

I have as little superstition in me as any man living, but my secret opinion has ever been, and still is, that God Almighty will not give up a people to military

---

* *The present winter is worth an age, if rightly employed; but, if lost or neglected, the whole continent will partake of the evil; and there is no punishment that man does not deserve, be he who, or what, or where he will, that may be the means of sacrificing a season so precious and useful.*

destruction, or leave them unsupportedly to perish, who have so earnestly and so repeatedly sought to avoid the calamities of war, by every decent method which wisdom could invent. Neither have I so much of the infidel in me, as to suppose that He has relinquished the government of the world, and given us up to the care of devils; and as I do not, I cannot see on what grounds the king of Britain can look up to heaven for help against us: a common murderer, a highwayman, or a housebreaker, has as good a pretence as he. . . .

As I was with the troops at Fort Lee, and marched with them to the edge of Pennsylvania, I am well acquainted with many circumstances, which those who live at a distance know but little or nothing of. Our situation there was exceedingly cramped, the place being a narrow neck of land between the North River and the Hackensack. Our force was inconsiderable, being not one fourth so great as Howe could bring against us. We had no army at hand to have relieved the garrison, had we shut ourselves up and stood on our defence. Our ammunition, light artillery, and the best part of our stores, had been removed, on the apprehension that Howe would endeavor to penetrate the Jerseys, in which case Fort Lee could be of no use to us; for it must occur to every thinking man, whether in the army or not, that these kind of field forts are only for temporary purposes, and last in use no longer than the enemy directs his force against the particular object, which such forts are raised to defend. Such was our situation and condition at fort Lee on the morning of the 20th of November, when an officer arrived with information that the enemy with 200 boats had landed about seven miles above: Major General Green, who commanded the garrison, immediately ordered them under arms, and sent express to General Washington at the town of Hackensack, distant by the way of the ferry = six miles. Our first object was to secure the bridge over the Hackensack, which laid up the river between the enemy and us, about six miles from us, and three from them. General Washington arrived in about three quarters of an hour, and marched at the head of the troops towards the bridge, which place I expected we should have a brush for; however, they did not choose to dispute it with us, and the greatest part of our troops went over the bridge, the rest over the ferry, except some which passed at a mill on a small creek, between the bridge and the ferry, and made their way through some marshy grounds up to the town of Hackensack, and there passed the river. We brought off as much baggage as the wagons could contain, the rest was lost. The simple object was to bring off the garrison, and march them on till they could be strengthened by the Jersey or Pennsylvania militia, so as to be enabled to make a stand. We staid four days at Newark, collected our out-posts with some of the Jersey militia, and marched out twice to meet the enemy, on being informed that they were advancing, though our numbers were greatly inferior to theirs. Howe, in my little opinion, committed a great error in generalship in not throwing a body of forces off from Staten Island through Amboy, by which means he might have seized all our stores at Brunswick, and intercepted our march into Pennsylvania; but if we believe the power of hell to be limited, we must likewise believe that their agents are under some providential controul.

I shall not now attempt to give all the particulars of our retreat to the Delaware; suffice it for the present to say, that both officers and men, though greatly harrassed and fatigued, frequently without rest, covering, or provision, the inevitable consequences of a long retreat, bore it with a manly and martial spirit. All their wishes centered in one, which was, that the country would turn out and help them to drive the enemy back. Voltaire has remarked that King William never appeared to full advantage but in difficulties and in action; the same remark may be made on General Washington, for the character fits him. There is a natural firmness in some minds which cannot be unlocked by trifles, but which, when unlocked, discovers a cabinet of fortitude; and I reckon it among those kind of public blessings, which we do not immediately see, that God hath blessed him with uninterrupted health, and given him a mind that can even flourish upon care.

I shall conclude this paper with some miscellaneous remarks on the state of our affairs; and shall begin with asking the following question, Why is it that the enemy have left the New-England provinces, and made these middle ones the seat of war? The answer is easy: New-England is not infested with tories, and we are. I have been tender in raising the cry against these men, and used numberless arguments to show them their danger, but it will not do to sacrifice a world either to their folly or their baseness. The period is now arrived, in which either they or we must change our sentiments, or one or both must fall. And what is a tory? Good God! what is he? I should not be afraid to go with a hundred whigs against a thousand tories, were they to attempt to get into arms. Every tory is a coward; for servile, slavish, self-interested fear is the foundation of toryism; and a man under such influence, though he may be cruel, never can be brave.

But, before the line of irrecoverable separation be drawn between us, let us reason the matter together: Your conduct is an invitation to the enemy, yet not one in a thousand of you has heart enough to join him. Howe is as much deceived by you as the American cause is injured by you. He expects you will all take up arms, and flock to his standard, with muskets on your shoulders. Your opinions are of no use to him, unless you support him personally, for 'tis soldiers, and not tories, that he wants.

I once felt all that kind of anger, which a man ought to feel, against the mean principles that are held by the tories: a noted one, who kept a tavern at Amboy, was standing at his door, with as pretty a child in his hand, about eight or nine years old, as ever I saw, and after speaking his mind as freely as he thought was prudent, finished with this unfatherly expression, *"Well! give me peace in my day."* Not a man lives on the continent but fully believes that a separation must some time or other finally take place, and a generous parent should have said, *"If there must be trouble, let it be in my day, that my child may have peace;"* and this single reflection, well applied, is sufficient to awaken every man to duty. Not a place upon earth might be so happy as America. Her situation is remote from all the wrangling world, and she has nothing to do but to trade with them. A man can distinguish himself between temper and principle, and I am as confident, as I am that God governs the world, that America will never be happy till she gets clear of foreign dominion. Wars, without ceasing, will break out till that period arrives, and the continent must in the end be conqueror; for though the flame of liberty may sometimes cease to shine, the coal can never expire . . .

William B. Cairns, ed., *Selections from Early American Writers*, 1607 1800 (New York: Macmillan, 1909).

6

The Declaration of Independence, July 4, 1776

The Declaration is the philosophical defense of the separation from England as well as a list of grievances that form the rationale for having our own go at things. Many founders wrote about the importance of government in securing happiness for its

people; it's important to realize that these
references are about the private citizen's right
to pursue happiness, not the role of the state
in providing for the happiness of its people—
especially at the expense of other citizens.

When in the Course of human events, it becomes necessary for one people to dissolve the political bands which have connected them with another, and to assume among the powers of the earth, the separate and equal station to which the Laws of Nature and of Nature's God entitle them, a decent respect to the opinions of mankind requires that they should declare the causes which impel them to the separation.

We hold these truths to be self-evident, that all

men are created equal, that they are endowed by their Creator with certain unalienable Rights, that among these are Life, Liberty, and the pursuit of Happiness.— That to secure these rights, Governments are instituted among Men, deriving their just powers from the consent of the governed,—that whenever any Form of Government becomes destructive of these ends, it is the Right of the People to alter or to abolish it, and to institute new Government, laying its foundation on such principles and organizing its powers in such form, as to them shall seem most likely to effect their Safety and Happiness. Prudence, indeed, will dictate that Governments long established should not be changed for light and transient causes; and accordingly all experience hath shewn, that mankind are more disposed to suffer, while evils are sufferable, than to right themselves by abolishing the forms to which they are accustomed. But when a long train of abuses and usurpations, pursuing invariably the same Object evinces a design to reduce them under absolute Despotism, it is their right, it is their duty, to throw off such Government, and to provide new Guards for their future security.—Such has been the patient sufferance of these Colonies; and such is now the necessity which constrains them to alter their former Systems of Government. The history of the present King of Great Britain is a history of repeated injuries and usurpations, all having in direct object the establishment of an absolute Tyranny over these States. To prove this, let Facts be submitted to a candid world.

He has refused his Assent to Laws, the most wholesome and necessary for the public good.

He has forbidden his Governors to pass

Laws of immediate and pressing importance, unless suspended in their operation till his Assent should be obtained; and when so suspended, he has utterly neglected to attend to them.

He has refused to pass other Laws for the accommodation of large districts of people, unless those people would relinquish the right of Representation in the Legislature, a right inestimable to them, and formidable to tyrants only.

He has called together legislative bodies at places unusual, uncomfortable, and distant from the depository of their public Records, for the sole purpose of fatiguing them into compliance with his measures.

He has dissolved Representative Houses repeatedly, for opposing with manly firmness his invasions on the rights of the people.

He has refused for a long time, after such dissolutions, to cause others to be elected; whereby the Legislative powers, incapable of Annihilation, have returned to the People at large for their exercise; the State remaining in the mean time exposed to all the dangers of invasion from without, and convulsions within.

He has endeavored to prevent the population of these States; for that purpose obstructing the Laws for Naturalization of Foreigners; refusing to pass others to encourage their migrations hither, and raising the conditions of new Appropriations of Lands.

He has obstructed the Administration of Justice, by refusing his Assent to Laws for establishing Judiciary powers.

He has made Judges dependent on his Will

alone, for the tenure of their offices, and the amount and payment of their salaries.

He has erected a multitude of New Offices, and sent hither swarms of Officers to harass our people, and eat out their substance.

He has kept among us, in times of peace, Standing Armies without the Consent of our legislatures.

He has affected to render the Military independent of and superior to the Civil power.

He has combined with others to subject us to a jurisdiction foreign to our constitution, and unacknowledged by our laws; giving his Assent to their Acts of pretended Legislation:

For Quartering large bodies of armed troops among us:

For protecting them, by a mock Trial, from

punishment for any Murders which they should commit on the Inhabitants of these States:

For cutting off our Trade with all parts of the world:

For imposing Taxes on us without our Consent:

For depriving us in many cases, of the benefits of Trial by Jury:

For transporting us beyond Seas to be tried for pretended offenses

For abolishing the free System of English Laws in a neighbouring Province, establishing therein an Arbitrary government, and enlarging its Boundaries so as to render it at once an example and fit instrument for introducing the same absolute rule into these Colonies:

For taking away our Charters, abolishing

our most valuable Laws, and altering fundamentally the Forms of our Governments:

For suspending our own Legislatures, and declaring themselves invested with power to legislate for us in all cases whatsoever.

He has abdicated Government here, by declaring us out of his Protection and waging War against us.

He has plundered our seas, ravaged our Coasts, burnt our towns, and destroyed the lives of our people.

He is at this time transporting large Armies of foreign Mercenaries to complete the works of death, desolation and tyranny, already begun with circumstances of Cruelty & perfidy scarcely paralleled in the most barbarous ages, and totally unworthy the Head of a civilized nation.

He has constrained our fellow Citizens taken Captive on the high Seas to bear Arms against their Country, to become the executioners of their friends and Brethren, or to fall themselves by their Hands.

He has excited domestic insurrections amongst us, and has endeavored to bring on the inhabitants of our frontiers, the merciless Indian Savages, whose known rule of warfare, is an undistinguished destruction of all ages, sexes and conditions.

In every stage of these Oppressions We have Petitioned for Redress in the most humble terms: Our repeated Petitions have been answered only by repeated injury. A Prince whose character is thus marked by every act which may define a Tyrant, is unfit to be the ruler of a free people.

Nor have We been wanting in our attentions to our British brethren. We have warned them from time to time of attempts by their legislature to extend an unwarrantable jurisdiction over us. We have reminded them of the circumstances of our emigration and settlement here. We have appealed to their native justice and magnanimity, and we have conjured them by the ties of our common kindred to disavow these usurpations, which, would inevitably interrupt our connections and correspondence. They too have been deaf to the voice of justice and of consanguinity. We must, therefore, acquiesce in the necessity, which denounces our Separation, and hold them, as we hold the rest of mankind, Enemies in War, in Peace Friends.

We, therefore, the Representatives of the united States of America, in General Congress, Assembled, appealing to the Supreme Judge of the world for the rectitude of our intentions, do, in the Name, and by Authority of the good People of these Colonies, solemnly publish and declare, That these United Colonies are, and of Right ought to be free and independent states; that they are Absolved from all Allegiance to the British Crown, and that all political connection between them and the State of Great Britain, is and ought to be totally dissolved; and that as Free and Independent States, they have full Power to levy War, conclude Peace, contract Alliances, establish Commerce, and to do all other Acts and Things which Independent States may of right do. And for the support of this Declaration, with a firm reliance on the protection of divine Providence, we mutually pledge to each other our Lives, our Fortunes and our sacred Honor.

[Signed by] John Hancock [President]

Georgia:
Button Gwinnett
Lyman Hall
George Walton

New Hampshire:
Josiah Bartlett
William Whipple
Matthew Thornton

North Carolina:
Wm. Hooper
Joseph Hewes
John Penn

South Carolina:
Edward Rutledge
Thomas Hayward,
  Jr.
Thomas Lynch, Jr.
Arthur Middleton

Maryland:
Samuel Chase
William Paca
Thomas Stone
Charles Carroll of
  Carrollton

Virginia:
George Wythe
Richard Henry Lee
Thomas Jefferson
Benjamin Harrison
Thomas Nelson, Jr.
Francis Lightfoot
  Lee
Carter Braxton

Pennsylvania:
Robert Morris
Benjamin Rush
Benjamin Franklin
John Morton
George Clymer
Jason Smith

George Taylor
James Wilson
George Ross

Delaware:
Caesar Rodney
George Read
Thomas M'Kean

New York:
William Floyd
Phillip Livingston
Francis Lewis
Lewis Morris

New Jersey:
Richard Stockton

John Witherspoon
Francis Hopkinson
John Hart
Abraham Clark

Massachusetts:
Samuel Adams
John Adams
Robert Treatpaine
Elbridge Gerry

Rhode Island:
Stephen Hopkins
William Ellery

Connecticut:
Roger Sherman
Samuel Huntington
William Williams
Oliver Wolcott

Mr. Ferdinand Jefferson, Keeper of the Rolls in the Department of State, at Washington, says: "The names of the signers are spelt above as in the facsimile of the original, but the punctuation of them is not always the same; neither do the names of the States appear in the facsimile of the original.

The names of the signers of each State are grouped together in the facsimile of the original, except the name of Matthew Thornton, which follows that of Oliver Wolcott."—Revised Statutes of the United States, 2nd ed., 1878.

---

www.archives.gov/exhibits/charters/declaration_transcript.html. Accessed February 17, 2010.

7

Thomas Paine's
Common Sense
(Selections)

*Published anonymously by Thomas Paine in
1776,* Common Sense—*using plain language
everyone could understand—became one of
the most influential writings of the American
Revolution. It advocated a declaration of
independence from Great Britain and stirred
the pot of rising revolutionary sentiment.*

Some writers have so confounded society with government, as to leave little or no distinction between them; whereas they are not only different, but have different origins. Society is produced by our wants, and government by our wickedness; the former promotes our happiness *positively*, by uniting our affections; the latter *negatively*, by restraining our vices. The one encourages intercourse, the other creates distinctions. The first is a patron, the last is a punisher.

Society in every state is a blessing, but government, even in its best state, is but a necessary evil; in its worst state, an intolerable one; for when we suffer, or are exposed to the same miseries *by a government*, which we might expect in a country *without government*, our calamity is heightened by reflecting that we furnish the means by which we suffer. Government, like dress, is the badge of lost innocence: the palaces of kings are built on the ruins of the bowers of paradise. For, were the impulses of conscience clear, uniform, and irresistibly obeyed, man would need no other lawgiver; but that not being the case, he finds it necessary to surrender up a part of his property to furnish means for the protection of the rest; and this he is induced to do by the same prudence which, in every other case, advises him out of two evils to choose the least. *Wherefore*, security being the true design and end of government, it unanswerably follows, that whatever *form* thereof appears most likely to ensure it to us with the least expense and greatest benefit, is preferable to all others. . . .

Oppression is often the *consequence*, but seldom or never the *means* of riches; and though avarice will preserve a man from being necessitously poor, it generally makes him too timorous to be wealthy.

But there is another and greater distinction, for which no truly natural or religious reason can be assigned, and that is, the distinction of men into KINGS and SUBJECTS. Male and female are the distinctions of nature, good and bad the distinctions of heaven; but how a race of men came into the world so exalted above the rest, and distinguished like some new species, is worth enquiring into, and whether they are the means of happiness or of misery to mankind. . . .

One of the strongest *natural* proofs of the folly of hereditary right of kings, is that nature disapproves it, otherwise she would not so frequently turn it into ridicule by giving mankind *an ass for a lion*. . . .

Every quiet method for peace hath been ineffectual. Our prayers have been rejected with disdain; and only tended to convince us that nothing flatters vanity, or confirms obstinacy in kings more than repeated petitioning—and nothing hath contributed more than this very measure to make the kings of Europe absolute. . . .

As to government matters, it is not in the power of Britain to do this continent justice: the business of it will soon be too weighty and intricate to be managed with any tolerable degree of convenience, by a power so distant from us, and so very ignorant of us; for if they cannot conquer us, they cannot govern us. . . .

O ye that love mankind! Ye that dare oppose, not only the tyranny, but the tyrant, stand forth! Every spot of the old world is overrun with oppression. Freedom hath been hunted round the globe. Asia and Africa have long expelled her, Europe regards her like a stranger, and England hath given her warning to depart. O! receive the fugitive, and prepare in time an asylum for mankind. . . .

Since the publication of the first edition of this pamphlet, or rather, on the same day on which it came out, the king's speech made its appearance in this city [Philadelphia]. Had the spirit of prophecy directed the birth of this production, it could not have brought it forth at a more seasonable juncture, or at a more necessary time. The bloody-mindedness of the one, shows the necessity of pursuing the doctrine of the other. Men read by way of revenge: and the speech, instead of terrifying, prepared a way for the manly principles of independence.

Thomas Paine, *Common Sense* (New York: Peter Eckler, 1918).

8

Thomas Jefferson on Decentralized Government and the Judiciary

In his Autobiography, *Thomas Jefferson remarked on the fact that the judicial branch of government should be independent of the other branches, but not independent of the people. Based on his observation that judges tend to expand their*

own powers, he felt they should be appointed
for limited terms and that their conduct on the
bench should affect their reappointments.

. . . It is not enough that honest men are appointed Judges. All know the influence of interest on the mind of man, and how unconsciously his judgment is warped by that influence. To this bias add that of the *esprit de corps*, of their peculiar maxim and creed, that "it is the office of a good Judge to enlarge his jurisdiction," and the absence of responsibility; and how can we expect impartial decision between the General government, of which they are themselves so eminent a part, and an individual State, from which they have nothing to hope or fear? We have seen, too, that contrary to all correct example, they are in the habit of going out of the question before them, to throw an anchor ahead, and grapple further hold for future advances of power. They are then, in fact, the corps of sappers and miners, steadily working to undermine the independent rights of the States, and to consolidate all power in the hands of that government in which they have so important a freehold estate. But it is not by the consolidation, or concentration of powers, but by their distribution, that good government is effected. Were not this great country already divided into States, that division must be made, that each might do for itself what concerns itself directly, and what it can so much better do than a distant authority. Every State again is divided into counties, each to take care of what lies within its local bounds; each county again into townships or wards, to manage minuter details; and every ward into farms, to be governed each by its individual proprietor. Were we directed from Washington when to sow, and when to reap, we should soon want bread. It is by this partition of cares, descending in gradation from general to particular, that the mass of human affairs may be best managed, for the good and prosperity of all. I repeat, that I do not charge the Judges with wilful and ill-intentioned error; but honest error must be arrested, where its toleration leads to public ruin. As, for the safety of society, we commit honest maniacs to Bedlam, so judges should be withdrawn from their bench, whose erroneous biases are leading us to dissolution. It may, indeed, injure them in fame or in fortune; but it saves the Republic, which is the first and supreme law.

H. A. Washington, ed., *The Writings of Thomas Jefferson*, vol. 1 (Washington, D.C.: Taylor & Maury, 1853).

9

Benjamin Franklin on the Pursuit of Power and Position

A sobering reminder of what drives many people into government, Franklin's observation, delivered at the Constitutional Convention in 1787, is not so much born of cynicism as it is realism and decades of experience.

Sir, there are two passions which have a powerful influence in the affairs of men. These are ambition and avarice; the love of power and the love of money. Separately, each of these has great force in prompting men to action; but, when united in view of the same object, they have, in many minds, the most violent effects. Place before the eyes of such men a post of honor, that shall, at the same time, be a place of profit, and they will move heaven and earth to obtain it. The vast number of such places it is that renders the British Government so tempestuous. The struggles for them are the true source of all those factions which are perpetually dividing the nation, distracting its councils, hurrying it sometimes into fruitless and mischievous wars, and often compelling a submission to dishonorable terms of peace.

And of what kind are the men that will strive

for this profitable pre-eminence, through all the bustle of cabal, the heat of contention, the infinite mutual abuse of parties, tearing to pieces the best of characters? It will not be the wise and moderate, the lovers of peace and good order, the men fittest for the trust. It will be the bold and the violent, the men of strong passions and indefatigable activity in their selfish pursuits. These will thrust themselves into your government, and be your rulers. And these, too, will be mistaken in the expected happiness of their situation, for their vanquished competitors, of the same spirit, and from the same motives, will perpetually be endeavoring to distress their administration, thwart their measures, and render them odious to the people.

Mayo Williamson Hazeltine, ed., *Orations from Homer to William McKinley*, vol. 5 (New York: P.F. Collier and Son, 1902).

10

The Constitution of the United States

After the Revolutionary War ended in 1783,
the states faced new problems. In peacetime
there were new issues that the Articles of
Confederation didn't adequately address: paying
a large public war debt, enforcing law and
order, regulating trade, dealing with Indian
tribes, and negotiating with other governments.
In May of 1787, the Federal Convention

convened in Philadelphia, where the delegates decided that rather than revising the Articles of Confederation, they would create a new and stronger Constitution. The debate lasted all summer as the founding fathers crafted a system of government that would define the rights and liberties of the American people and provide for three branches of government, none of which would have dominance over the others. The Constitution was first ratified on December 7, 1787, by Delaware and went into effect on June 11, 1788, when New Hampshire ratified it. It has since been amended twenty-seven times, including the Bill of Rights. This is the original version of the Constitution; we've italicized portions that were later amended or suspended.

WE THE PEOPLE of the United States, in Order to form a more perfect Union, establish Justice, insure domestic Tranquility, provide for the common defence, promote the general Welfare, and secure the Blessings of Liberty to ourselves and our Posterity, do ordain and establish this Constitution for the United States of America.

ARTICLE. I.

Section. 1.

All legislative Powers herein granted shall be vested in a Congress of the United States, which shall consist of a Senate and House of Representatives.

Section. 2.

The House of Representatives shall be composed of Members chosen every second Year by the People of the several States, and the Electors in each State shall have the Qualifications requisite for Electors of the most numerous Branch of the State Legislature.

No Person shall be a Representative who shall not have attained to the Age of twenty five Years, and been seven Years a Citizen of the United States, and who shall not, when elected, be an Inhabitant of that State in which he shall be chosen.

Representatives and direct Taxes shall be apportioned among the several States which may be included within this Union, according to their respective Numbers, which shall be determined by adding to the whole Number of free Persons, including those bound to Service for a Term of Years, and excluding Indians not taxed, three fifths of all other Persons. The actual Enumeration shall be made within three Years after the first Meeting of the Congress of the United States, and within every subsequent Term of ten Years, in such Manner as they shall by Law direct. The Number of Representatives shall not exceed one for every thirty Thousand, but each State shall have at Least one Representative; and until such enumeration shall be made, the State of New Hampshire shall be entitled to chuse three, Massachusetts eight, Rhode-Island and Providence Plantations one, Connecticut five, New-York six, New Jersey four, Pennsylvania eight, Delaware one, Maryland six, Virginia ten, North Carolina five, South Carolina five, and Georgia three.

When vacancies happen in the Representation from any State, the Executive Authority thereof shall issue Writs of Election to fill such Vacancies.

The House of Representatives shall chuse their Speaker and other Officers; and shall have the sole Power of Impeachment.

Section. 3.

The Senate of the United States shall be composed of two Senators from each State, *chosen by the Legislature* thereof for six Years; and each Senator shall have one Vote.

Immediately after they shall be assembled in Consequence of the first Election, they shall be divided as equally as may be into three Classes. The Seats of the Senators of the first Class shall be vacated at the Expiration of the second Year, of the second Class at the Expiration of the fourth Year, and of the third Class at the Expiration of the sixth Year, so that one third may be chosen every second Year; *and if Vacancies happen by Resignation, or otherwise, during the Recess of the Legislature of any State, the Executive thereof may make temporary Appointments until the next Meeting of the Legislature, which shall then fill such Vacancies.*

No Person shall be a Senator who shall not have attained to the Age of thirty Years, and been nine Years a Citizen of the United States, and who shall not, when elected, be an Inhabitant of that State for which he shall be chosen.

The Vice President of the United States shall be President of the Senate, but shall have no Vote, unless they be equally divided.

The Senate shall chuse their other Officers, and also a President pro tempore, in the Absence of the Vice President, or when he shall exercise the Office of President of the United States.

The Senate shall have the sole Power to try all

Impeachments. When sitting for that Purpose, they shall be on Oath or Affirmation. When the President of the United States is tried, the Chief Justice shall preside: And no Person shall be convicted without the Concurrence of two thirds of the Members present.

Judgment in Cases of Impeachment shall not extend further than to removal from Office, and disqualification to hold and enjoy any Office of honor, Trust or Profit under the United States: but the Party convicted shall nevertheless be liable and subject to Indictment, Trial, Judgment and Punishment, according to Law.

Section. 4.

The Times, Places and Manner of holding Elections for Senators and Representatives, shall be prescribed in each State by the Legislature thereof;

but the Congress may at any time by Law make or alter such Regulations, except as to the Places of chusing Senators.

The Congress shall assemble at least once in every Year, and such Meeting shall *be on the first Monday in December*, unless they shall by Law appoint a different Day.

Section. 5.

Each House shall be the Judge of the Elections, Returns and Qualifications of its own Members, and a Majority of each shall constitute a Quorum to do Business; but a smaller Number may adjourn from day to day, and may be authorized to compel the Attendance of absent Members, in such Manner, and under such Penalties as each House may provide.

Each House may determine the Rules of its Proceedings, punish its Members for disorderly Behaviour, and, with the Concurrence of two thirds, expel a Member.

Each House shall keep a Journal of its Proceedings, and from time to time publish the same, excepting such Parts as may in their Judgment require Secrecy; and the Yeas and Nays of the Members of either House on any question shall, at the Desire of one fifth of those Present, be entered on the Journal.

Neither House, during the Session of Congress, shall, without the Consent of the other, adjourn for more than three days, nor to any other Place than that in which the two Houses shall be sitting.

Section. 6.

The Senators and Representatives shall receive a

Compensation for their Services, to be ascertained by Law, and paid out of the Treasury of the United States. They shall in all Cases, except Treason, Felony and Breach of the Peace, be privileged from Arrest during their Attendance at the Session of their respective Houses, and in going to and returning from the same; and for any Speech or Debate in either House, they shall not be questioned in any other Place.

No Senator or Representative shall, during the Time for which he was elected, be appointed to any civil Office under the Authority of the United States, which shall have been created, or the Emoluments whereof shall have been encreased during such time; and no Person holding any Office under the United States, shall be a Member of either House during his Continuance in Office.

Section. 7.

All Bills for raising Revenue shall originate in the House of Representatives; but the Senate may propose or concur with Amendments as on other Bills.

Every Bill which shall have passed the House of Representatives and the Senate, shall, before it become a Law, be presented to the President of the United States: If he approve he shall sign it, but if not he shall return it, with his Objections to that House in which it shall have originated, who shall enter the Objections at large on their Journal, and proceed to reconsider it. If after such Reconsideration two thirds of that House shall agree to pass the Bill, it shall be sent, together with the Objections, to the other House, by which it shall likewise be reconsidered, and if approved by two thirds of that House, it shall become a Law. But in all such Cases the Votes of both Houses shall be determined by yeas and Nays, and the Names of the Persons voting for and against the Bill shall be entered on the Journal of each House respectively. If any Bill shall not be returned by the President within ten Days (Sundays excepted) after it shall have been presented to him, the Same shall be a Law, in like Manner as if he had signed it, unless the Congress by their Adjournment prevent its Return, in which Case it shall not be a Law.

Every Order, Resolution, or Vote to which the Concurrence of the Senate and House of Representatives may be necessary (except on a question of Adjournment) shall be presented to the President of the United States; and before the Same shall take Effect, shall be approved by him, or being disapproved by him, shall be repassed by two thirds of the Senate and House of Representatives, according to the Rules and Limitations prescribed in the Case of a Bill.

Section. 8.

The Congress shall have Power To lay and collect Taxes, Duties, Imposts and Excises, to pay the Debts and provide for the common Defence and general Welfare of the United States; but all Duties, Imposts and Excises shall be uniform throughout the United States;

To borrow Money on the credit of the United States;

To regulate Commerce with foreign Nations, and among the several States, and with the Indian Tribes;

To establish an uniform Rule of Naturalization, and uniform Laws on the subject of Bankruptcies throughout the United States;

To coin Money, regulate the Value thereof, and of

foreign Coin, and fix the Standard of Weights and Measures;

To provide for the Punishment of counterfeiting the Securities and current Coin of the United States;

To establish Post Offices and post Roads;

To promote the Progress of Science and useful Arts, by securing for limited Times to Authors and Inventors the exclusive Right to their respective Writings and Discoveries;

To constitute Tribunals inferior to the supreme Court;

To define and punish Piracies and Felonies committed on the high Seas, and Offences against the Law of Nations;

To declare War, grant Letters of Marque and Reprisal, and make Rules concerning Captures on Land and Water;

To raise and support Armies, but no Appropriation of Money to that Use shall be for a longer Term than two Years;

To provide and maintain a Navy;

To make Rules for the Government and Regulation of the land and naval Forces;

To provide for calling forth the Militia to execute the Laws of the Union, suppress Insurrections and repel Invasions;

To provide for organizing, arming, and disciplining, the Militia, and for governing such Part of them as may be employed in the Service of the United States, reserving to the States respectively, the Appointment of the Officers, and the Authority of training the Militia according to the discipline prescribed by Congress;

To exercise exclusive Legislation in all Cases

whatsoever, over such District (not exceeding ten Miles square) as may, by Cession of particular States, and the Acceptance of Congress, become the Seat of the Government of the United States, and to exercise like Authority over all Places purchased by the Consent of the Legislature of the State in which the Same shall be, for the Erection of Forts, Magazines, Arsenals, dock-Yards, and other needful Buildings;—And

To make all Laws which shall be necessary and proper for carrying into Execution the foregoing Powers, and all other Powers vested by this Constitution in the Government of the United States, or in any Department or Officer thereof.

Section. 9.

The Migration or Importation of such Persons as any of the States now existing shall think proper to admit, shall not be prohibited by the Congress prior to the Year one thousand eight hundred and eight, but a Tax or duty may be imposed on such Importation, not exceeding ten dollars for each Person.

The Privilege of the Writ of Habeas Corpus shall not be suspended, unless when in Cases of Rebellion or Invasion the public Safety may require it.

No Bill of Attainder or ex post facto Law shall be passed.

No Capitation, or other direct, Tax shall be laid, *unless in Proportion to the Census or enumeration herein before directed to be taken.*

No Tax or Duty shall be laid on Articles exported from any State.

No Preference shall be given by any Regulation of Commerce or Revenue to the Ports of one State over those of another; nor shall Vessels bound to, or from, one State, be obliged to enter, clear, or pay Duties in another.

No Money shall be drawn from the Treasury, but in Consequence of Appropriations made by Law; and a regular Statement and Account of the Receipts and Expenditures of all public Money shall be published from time to time.

No Title of Nobility shall be granted by the United States: And no Person holding any Office of Profit or Trust under them, shall, without the Consent of the Congress, accept of any present, Emolument, Office, or Title, of any kind whatever, from any King, Prince, or foreign State.

Section. 10.

No State shall enter into any Treaty, Alliance, or Confederation; grant Letters of Marque and

Reprisal; coin Money; emit Bills of Credit; make any Thing but gold and silver Coin a Tender in Payment of Debts; pass any Bill of Attainder, ex post facto Law, or Law impairing the Obligation of Contracts, or grant any Title of Nobility.

No State shall, without the Consent of the Congress, lay any Imposts or Duties on Imports or Exports, except what may be absolutely necessary for executing it's inspection Laws: and the net Produce of all Duties and Imposts, laid by any State on Imports or Exports, shall be for the Use of the Treasury of the United States; and all such Laws shall be subject to the Revision and Controul of the Congress.

No State shall, without the Consent of Congress, lay any Duty of Tonnage, keep Troops, or Ships of War in time of Peace, enter into any Agreement or Compact with another State, or with a foreign Power, or engage in War, unless actually invaded, or in such imminent Danger as will not admit of delay.

ARTICLE. II.

Section. 1.

The executive Power shall be vested in a President of the United States of America. He shall hold his Office during the Term of four Years, and, together with the Vice President, chosen for the same Term, be elected, as follows:

Each State shall appoint, in such Manner as the Legislature thereof may direct, a Number of Electors, equal to the whole Number of Senators and Representatives to which the State may be entitled in the Congress: but no Senator or Representative, or

Person holding an Office of Trust or Profit under the United States, shall be appointed an Elector.

The Electors shall meet in their respective States, and vote by Ballot for two Persons, of whom one at least shall not be an Inhabitant of the same State with themselves. And they shall make a List of all the Persons voted for, and of the Number of Votes for each; which List they shall sign and certify, and transmit sealed to the Seat of the Government of the United States, directed to the President of the Senate. The President of the Senate shall, in the Presence of the Senate and House of Representatives, open all the Certificates, and the Votes shall then be counted. The Person having the greatest Number of Votes shall be the President, if such Number be a Majority of the whole Number of Electors appointed; and if there be more than one who have such Majority, and have an equal Number of Votes, then the House of Representatives shall immediately chuse by Ballot one of them for President; and if no Person have a Majority, then from the five highest on the List the said House shall in like Manner chuse the President. But in chusing the President, the Votes shall be taken by States, the Representation from each State having one Vote; A quorum for this purpose shall consist of a Member or Members from two thirds of the States, and a Majority of all the States shall be necessary to a Choice. In every Case, after the Choice of the President, the Person having the greatest Number of Votes of the Electors shall be the Vice President. But if there should remain two or more who have equal Votes, the Senate shall chuse from them by Ballot the Vice President.

The Congress may determine the Time of chusing the Electors, and the Day on which they shall give their Votes; which Day shall be the same throughout the United States.

No Person except a natural born Citizen, or a Citizen of the United States, at the time of the Adoption of this Constitution, shall be eligible to the Office of President; neither shall any Person be eligible to that Office who shall not have attained to the Age of thirty five Years, and been fourteen Years a Resident within the United States.

In Case of the Removal of the President from Office, or of his Death, Resignation, or Inability to discharge the Powers and Duties of the said Office, the Same shall devolve on the Vice President, and the Congress may by Law provide for the Case of Removal, Death, Resignation or Inability, both of the President and Vice President, declaring what Officer shall then act as President, and such Officer shall act accordingly, until the Disability be removed, or a President shall be elected.

The President shall, at stated Times, receive for

his Services, a Compensation, which shall neither be increased nor diminished during the Period for which he shall have been elected, and he shall not receive within that Period any other Emolument from the United States, or any of them.

Before he enter on the Execution of his Office, he shall take the following Oath or Affirmation:—"I do solemnly swear (or affirm) that I will faithfully execute the Office of President of the United States, and will to the best of my Ability, preserve, protect and defend the Constitution of the United States."

Section. 2.

The President shall be Commander in Chief of the Army and Navy of the United States, and of the Militia of the several States, when called into the actual Service of the United States; he may require the Opinion, in writing, of the principal Officer in each of the executive Departments, upon any Subject relating to the Duties of their respective Offices, and he shall have Power to grant Reprieves and Pardons for Offences against the United States, except in Cases of Impeachment.

He shall have Power, by and with the Advice and Consent of the Senate, to make Treaties, provided two thirds of the Senators present concur; and he shall nominate, and by and with the Advice and Consent of the Senate, shall appoint Ambassadors, other public Ministers and Consuls, Judges of the supreme Court, and all other Officers of the United States, whose Appointments are not herein otherwise provided for, and which shall be established by Law: but the Congress may by Law vest the Appointment of such inferior Officers, as they think proper, in the President alone, in the Courts of Law, or in the Heads of Departments.

The President shall have Power to fill up all Vacancies that may happen during the Recess of the Senate, by granting Commissions which shall expire at the End of their next Session.

Section. 3.

He shall from time to time give to the Congress Information of the State of the Union, and recommend to their Consideration such Measures as he shall judge necessary and expedient; he may, on extraordinary Occasions, convene both Houses, or either of them, and in Case of Disagreement between them, with Respect to the Time of Adjournment, he may adjourn them to such Time as he shall think proper; he shall receive Ambassadors and other public Ministers; he shall take Care that the Laws be faithfully executed, and shall Commission all the Officers of the United States.

Section. 4.

The President, Vice President and all civil Officers of the United States, shall be removed from Office on Impeachment for, and Conviction of, Treason, Bribery, or other high Crimes and Misdemeanors.

ARTICLE. III.

Section. 1.

The judicial Power of the United States shall be vested in one supreme Court, and in such inferior Courts as the Congress may from time to time ordain and establish. The Judges, both of the supreme and inferior Courts, shall hold their Offices during good Behaviour, and shall, at stated Times, receive for their Services a Compensation, which shall not be diminished during their Continuance in Office.

Section. 2.

The judicial Power shall extend to all Cases, in Law and Equity, arising under this Constitution, the Laws of the United States, and Treaties made, or which shall be made, under their Authority;—to all Cases affecting Ambassadors, other public Ministers and Consuls;—to all Cases of admiralty and maritime Jurisdiction;—to Controversies to which the United States shall be a Party;—to Controversies between two or more States;—*between a State and Citizens of another State,*—between Citizens of different States,—between Citizens of the same State claiming Lands under Grants of different States, and between a State, or the Citizens thereof, and foreign States, Citizens or Subjects.

In all Cases affecting Ambassadors, other public Ministers and Consuls, and those in which a State shall be Party, the supreme Court shall have original Jurisdiction. In all the other Cases before mentioned, the supreme Court shall have appellate Jurisdiction, both as to Law and Fact, with such Exceptions, and under such Regulations as the Congress shall make.

The Trial of all Crimes, except in Cases of Impeachment, shall be by Jury; and such Trial shall be held in the State where the said Crimes shall have been committed; but when not committed within any State, the Trial shall be at such Place or Places as the Congress may by Law have directed.

Section. 3.

Treason against the United States, shall consist only in levying War against them, or in adhering to their Enemies, giving them Aid and Comfort. No Person shall be convicted of Treason unless on the Testimony of two Witnesses to the same overt Act, or on Confession in open Court.

The Congress shall have Power to declare the Punishment of Treason, but no Attainder of Treason shall work Corruption of Blood, or Forfeiture except during the Life of the Person attainted.

ARTICLE. IV.

Section. 1.

Full Faith and Credit shall be given in each State

to the public Acts, Records, and judicial Proceedings of every other State. And the Congress may by general Laws prescribe the Manner in which such Acts, Records and Proceedings shall be proved, and the Effect thereof.

Section. 2.

The Citizens of each State shall be entitled to all Privileges and Immunities of Citizens in the several States.

A Person charged in any State with Treason, Felony, or other Crime, who shall flee from Justice, and be found in another State, shall on Demand of the executive Authority of the State from which he fled, be delivered up, to be removed to the State having Jurisdiction of the Crime.

No Person held to Service or Labour in one State,

under the Laws thereof, escaping into another, shall, in Consequence of any Law or Regulation therein, be discharged from such Service or Labour, but shall be delivered up on Claim of the Party to whom such Service or Labour may be due.

Section. 3.

New States may be admitted by the Congress into this Union; but no new State shall be formed or erected within the Jurisdiction of any other State; nor any State be formed by the Junction of two or more States, or Parts of States, without the Consent of the Legislatures of the States concerned as well as of the Congress.

The Congress shall have Power to dispose of and make all needful Rules and Regulations respecting the Territory or other Property belonging to the

United States; and nothing in this Constitution shall be so construed as to Prejudice any Claims of the United States, or of any particular State.

Section. 4.

The United States shall guarantee to every State in this Union a Republican Form of Government, and shall protect each of them against Invasion; and on Application of the Legislature, or of the Executive (when the Legislature cannot be convened), against domestic Violence.

ARTICLE. V.

The Congress, whenever two thirds of both Houses shall deem it necessary, shall propose Amendments to this Constitution, or, on the Application of the Legislatures of two thirds of the several States, shall call a Convention for proposing Amendments, which, in either Case, shall be valid to all Intents and Purposes, as Part of this Constitution, when ratified by the Legislatures of three fourths of the several States, or by Conventions in three fourths thereof, as the one or the other Mode of Ratification may be proposed by the Congress; Provided that no Amendment which may be made prior to the Year One thousand eight hundred and eight shall in any Manner affect the first and fourth Clauses in the Ninth Section of the first Article; and that no State, without its Consent, shall be deprived of its equal Suffrage in the Senate.

ARTICLE. VI.

All Debts contracted and Engagements entered into, before the Adoption of this Constitution, shall be as valid against the United States under this Constitution, as under the Confederation.

This Constitution, and the Laws of the United States which shall be made in Pursuance thereof; and all Treaties made, or which shall be made, under the Authority of the United States, shall be the supreme Law of the Land; and the Judges in every State shall be bound thereby, any Thing in the Constitution or Laws of any State to the Contrary notwithstanding.

The Senators and Representatives before mentioned, and the Members of the several State Legislatures, and all executive and judicial Officers, both of the United States and of the several States, shall be bound by Oath or Affirmation, to support this Constitution; but no religious Test shall ever be required as a Qualification to any Office or public Trust under the United States.

ARTICLE. VII.

The Ratification of the Conventions of nine States, shall be sufficient for the Establishment of this Constitution between the States so ratifying the Same.

The Word, "the," being interlined between the seventh and eighth Lines of the first Page, the Word "Thirty" being partly written on an Erazure in the fifteenth Line of the first Page, The Words "is tried" being interlined between the thirty second and thirty third Lines of the first Page and the Word "the" being interlined between the forty third and forty fourth Lines of the second Page.

Attest William Jackson Secretary

Done in Convention by the Unanimous Consent of the States present the Seventeenth Day of September in the Year of our Lord one thousand seven hundred and Eighty seven and of the Independence of the United States of America the Twelfth In witness whereof We have hereunto subscribed our Names,

G°. Washington
Presidt and deputy from Virginia

Delaware   John Dickinson
Geo: Read   Richard Bassett
Gunning Bedford jun   Jaco: Broom

Maryland

James McHenry

Dan of St Thos.
   Jenifer

Danl. Carroll

Virginia

John Blair

James Madison Jr.

North Carolina

Wm. Blount

Richd. Dobbs
   Spaight

Hu Williamson

South Carolina

J. Rutledge

Charles Cotesworth
   Pinckney

Charles Pinckney

Pierce Butler

Georgia

William Few

Abr Baldwin

New Hampshire

John Langdon

Nicholas Gilman

Massachusetts
Nathaniel Gorham
Rufus King

David Brearley
Wm. Paterson
Jona: Dayton

Connecticut
Wm. Saml. Johnson
Roger Sherman

Pennsylvania
B Franklin
Thomas Mifflin
Robt. Morris

New York
Alexander Hamilton

Geo. Clymer
Thos. FitzSimons
Jared Ingersoll

New Jersey
Wil: Livingston

James Wilson
Gouv Morris

---

www.archives.gov/exhibits/charters/constitution.html. Accessed December 21, 2009.

11

The Bill of Rights

By 1789 the United States Constitution had already been ratified, but many of the founding fathers—with fresh memories of the British violations of their human and civil rights—were wary of the potential tyranny of a strong central government. They demanded a "bill of rights" to protect the rights of the citizens. On December 15, 1791, the first ten amendments to the Constitution, known as the Bill of Rights, were ratified.

THE PREAMBLE TO THE
BILL OF RIGHTS

Congress of the United States begun and held at the City of New-York, on Wednesday the fourth of March, one thousand seven hundred and eighty nine.

THE Conventions of a number of the States, having at the time of their adopting the Constitution, expressed a desire, in order to prevent misconstruction or abuse of its powers, that further declaratory and restrictive clauses should be added: And as extending the ground of public confidence in the Government, will best ensure the beneficent ends of its institution.

RESOLVED by the Senate and House of Representatives of the United States of America, in Congress assembled, two thirds of both Houses concurring, that the following Articles be proposed to the Legislatures of the several States, as amendments to the Constitution of the United States, all, or any of which Articles, when ratified by three fourths of the said Legislatures, to be valid to all intents and purposes, as part of the said Constitution; viz.

ARTICLES in addition to, and Amendment of the Constitution of the United States of America, proposed by Congress, and ratified by the Legislatures of the several States, pursuant to the fifth Article of the original Constitution.

Amendment I

Congress shall make no law respecting an establishment of religion, or prohibiting the free exercise thereof; or abridging the freedom of speech, or of the press; or the right of the people peaceably to assemble, and to petition the Government for a redress of grievances.

Amendment II

A well regulated Militia, being necessary to the security of a free State, the right of the people to keep and bear Arms, shall not be infringed.

Amendment III

No Soldier shall, in time of peace be quartered in any house, without the consent of the Owner, nor in time of war, but in a manner to be prescribed by law.

Amendment IV

The right of the people to be secure in their persons, houses, papers, and effects, against unreasonable searches and seizures, shall not be violated, and no Warrants shall issue, but upon probable cause, supported by Oath or affirmation, and particularly describing the place to be searched, and the persons or things to be seized.

Amendment V

No person shall be held to answer for a capital, or otherwise infamous crime, unless on a presentment or indictment of a Grand Jury, except in cases arising in the land or naval forces, or in the Militia, when in actual service in time of War or public danger; nor shall any person be subject for the same offence to be twice put in jeopardy of life or limb; nor shall be compelled in any criminal case to be a witness against himself, nor be deprived of life, liberty, or property, without due process of law; nor shall private property be taken for public use, without just compensation.

Amendment VI

In all criminal prosecutions, the accused shall enjoy the right to a speedy and public trial, by an impartial jury of the State and district wherein the crime shall have been committed, which district shall have been previously ascertained by law, and to be informed of the nature and cause of the accusation; to be confronted with the witnesses against him; to have compulsory process for obtaining witnesses in his favor, and to have the Assistance of Counsel for his defence.

Amendment VII

In Suits at common law, where the value in controversy shall exceed twenty dollars, the right of trial by jury shall be preserved, and no fact tried by a jury, shall be otherwise re-examined in any Court of the

United States, than according to the rules of the common law.

Amendment VIII

Excessive bail shall not be required, nor excessive fines imposed, nor cruel and unusual punishments inflicted.

Amendment IX

The enumeration in the Constitution, of certain rights, shall not be construed to deny or disparage others retained by the people.

Amendment X

The powers not delegated to the United States by the Constitution, nor prohibited by it to the States, are reserved to the States respectively, or to the people.

www.archives.gov/exhibits/charters/bill_of_rights.html. Accessed December 21, 2009.

12

The First Inaugural Address of Thomas Jefferson, Delivered at Washington, D.C., March 4, 1801

When Chief Justice John Marshall administered the executive oath of office to Thomas Jefferson in 1801, it was the first time an inauguration was held in Washington, D.C. The outcome of the election had been hard fought, because Jefferson and Aaron Burr had tied in the electoral college. It took a special session of the House of Representatives, in a thirty-hour debate and balloting, to give Jefferson the win. Burr became vice president.

Friends And Fellow-citizens: Called upon to undertake the duties of the first executive office of our country, I avail myself of the presence of that portion of my fellow-citizens which is here assembled to express my grateful thanks for the favor with which they have been pleased to look toward me, to declare a sincere consciousness that the task is above my talents, and that I approach it with those anxious and awful presentiments which the greatness of the charge and the weakness of my powers so justly inspire. A rising nation, spread over a wide and fruitful land, traversing all the seas with the rich productions of their industry, engaged in commerce with nations who feel power and forget right, advancing rapidly to destinies beyond the reach of mortal eye—when I contemplate these transcendent objects, and see the honor, the happiness, and the hopes of this beloved country committed to the issue and the auspices of this day, I shrink from the contemplation, and humble myself before the magnitude of the undertaking. . . .

Sometimes it is said that man cannot be trusted with the government of himself. Can he, then, be trusted with the government of others? Or have we found angels in the forms of kings to govern him? Let history answer this question. . . .

Still one thing more, fellow-citizens—a wise and frugal Government, which shall restrain men from injuring one another, shall leave them otherwise free to regulate their own pursuits of industry and improvement, and shall not take from the mouth of labor the bread it has earned. This is the sum of good government, and this is necessary to close the circle of our felicities. . . .

Relying, then, on the patronage of your good-will, I advance with obedience to the work, ready to retire from it whenever you become sensible how much better choice it is in your power to make. And may that Infinite Power which rules the destinies of the universe lead our councils to what is best, and give them a favorable issue for your peace and prosperity.

Norman Foerster and William Whatley Pierson, eds., *American Ideals* (Houghton Mifflin Co., 1917).

13

Noah Webster's Oration on the Anniversary of the Declaration of Independence

In this cautionary offering on the twenty-sixth anniversary of the Declaration, Noah Webster warns America about those who would advance their own interests through the political system and by pandering to the people, even seducing and deceiving them. As a corrective, Webster points us to the values and examples of the patriots who have gone before.

Nations, like individuals, may be misled by an ardent enthusiasm, which allures them from the standard of practical wisdom, and commits them to the guidance of visionary projectors. By fondly cherishing the opinion that they enjoy some superior advantages of knowledge, or local situation, the rulers of a state may lose the benefit of history and observation, the surest guides in political affairs; and delude themselves with the belief, that they have wisdom to elude or power to surmount the obstacles which have baffled the exertions of their predecessors. . . .

If Moses, with an uncommon portion of talents, seconded by divine aid, could not secure his institutions from neglect and corruption, what right have we to expect, that the labors of our lawgivers will be more successful? . . .

The passions of men being every where the same, and nearly the same proportion of men in every society, directing their views to preferment, we observe that, in all governments, the object and efforts are the same, but the direction of those efforts is varied, according to the form of government, and *always applied to those who have the disposal of honors and offices.* In a monarchy, office-seekers are courtiers, fawning about the ministers or heads of departments. . . . in a pure democracy, they are orators, who mount the rostrum, and harangue the populace, flattering their pride, and inflaming their passions. . . .

in a representative republic, they are the *friends of the people*, who address themselves to the electors, with great pretensions to patriotism, with falsehoods, fair promises, and insidious arts. . . .

Whatever may be the form of government, therefore, corruption and misrepresentation find access to those who have the disposal of offices; by various means and different channels indeed, but proceeding primarily from demagogues and office-seekers, of bold designs and profligate principles.

It is said, however, that we have constitutions of government, or fundamental compacts, which proscribe abuses of power, by defining the exact limits of right and duty, and controlling both rulers and people. But how long will a constitutional barrier resist the assaults of faction? . . . When a magistrate becomes more popular than the constitution, he may "draw sin as it were with a cart-rope" in the work of extending his power over the instrument which was intended to restrain usurpation.* Whatever vanity and self-confidence may suggest, in favor of the restraints of a paper compact, all history and uniform experience evince, that against men who command the current of popular confidence, the best constitution has not the strength of a cobweb. The undisguised encroachments of power give the alarm and excite resistance. . . . but the approaches of despotism, under cover of popular favor, are insidious and often deceive the most discerning friends of a free government. . . .

To be a tyrant with any tolerable degree of safety, a man must be fully possessed of the confidence of the *people*. . . .

The open advocate of a strong government is

---

* Editor's Note: Webster is here quoting from Isaiah 5:18, a passage pronouncing woe upon the unjust and those who "call evil good, and good evil" (v. 20).

subject to popular odium, his encroachments are eyed with jealousy, or resisted by force. But the hypocritical pretender to patriotism acquires, in the confidence of the people, a giant's force, and he may use it like a giant. The people, like artless females, are liable to be seduced, not by the men they hate or suspect, but by those they love. . . .

A republican government, in which the supreme power is created by choice, is unquestionably the most excellent form of government in theory. . . .

But although a republican government is admitted to be the best, and most congenial to our state of society, its innate perfections and unavoidable abuses, render it far less durable, than its enthusiastic admirers have supposed. This conclusion, drawn from experience, should silence the complaints of men, who look for more perfection in government than it is susceptible of receiving; it should allay the animosities and temper the discussions of our citizens;. . . . it should produce a more indulgent spirit towards the faults of men in power and the errors of private individuals.

The consideration, also, that the intended effects of a free government, are mostly defeated by an abuse of its privileges, should make us more solicitous to acquire a deep and correct knowledge of its true principles, and more vigilant in guarding against the impositions of designing men. . . . men who seek offices by fair promises, and flatter only to deceive. Most men are more willing to command than to obey. . . . and more men are desirous to obtain public favor, than are willing to deserve it, by severe study and laborious services. One truth, also, ought to be deeply impressed on the minds of freemen, that men of real worth are always the last to seek offices for themselves. . . . and the last to clamor against men of worth who possess them. . . .

Let the youth of our country, who were not spectators of the distresses of the war; but who have entered upon the stage of life in time to see the silver locks of the revolutionary patriots, and to witness the scars and the poverty of the war-worn soldier. . . . let these ponder the history and listen to the tale of their fathers' sufferings, and their country's danger. Let them read the animated and energetic addresses of the first American Congress, whose firmness and eloquence would have honored a Roman Senate . . . Let them early imbibe the manly and dignified sentiments of that illustrious council which pointed out the road to independence . . . Let them catch a portion of the patriotic flame . . . and by learning to revere the sentiments, may they be led to follow the example, of those venerable sages. . . . Let them review, in imagination, the heroic achievements of the American troops. . . . Let them see, at Bunker's hill, a few hardy farmers, twice repulsing the numerous, well-marshalled columns of the foe, and holding the issue of the contest in suspense. . . . Let them transport their imaginations to the hills of Bennington, the fields of Saratoga, the almost inaccessible cliffs of Stony Point, and the plains of Yorktown where the armies of America closed their triumphs; there let them admire the heroism of the citizen soldier, and catch the spirit of victory. Then let them cast their eyes upon a shattered army, retreating before a triumphant foe. . . . See the magnanimous WASHINGTON, almost deserted and driven to despair, rallying a small band of half-clothed, dispirited troops, whose naked feet, lacerated with the frost bound clods, stained the road with blood, as they marched to the victories of Trenton and Princeton! Let scenes like these lead them to compassionate the distresses of a half-famished soldiery, who suffered and bled to defend the blessings which we now enjoy, and whose services are yet unrewarded. And when our youth see a needy soldier, grown old in poverty, or the widows and orphans of soldiers, doomed to want by the loss of their protectors, and the depreciation of government paper, let them open the liberal hand of bounty, and by relieving their wants, still divide with them the burthens and the distresses of the revolution. Let them consider that upon them has devolved the task of defending and improving the rich inheritance, purchased by their fathers. Nor let them view this inheritance of National Freedom and Independence, as a fortune that is to be squandered away, in ease and riot, but as an estate to be preserved only by industry, toil and vigilance. Let them cast their eyes around upon the aged fathers of the land, whose declining strength calls for their support, and whose venerable years and wisdom demand their deference and respect. Let them view the fair daughters of America, whose blushing cheeks and modest deportment invite their friendship and protection; whose virtues they are to cherish and reward by their love and fidelity; and whose honor and happiness it is their duty to maintain inviolable. Let them learn to merit the esteem and affections of females of worth, whose rank in life depends much on the reputation of their husbands, and who therefore never fail to respect men of character, as much as they despise those who waste their lives in idleness, gaming and frivolous pursuits.

And let us pay the tribute of respect to the memory of the illustrious hero who led our armies in the field of victory, and the statesman who first presided over our national councils. Let us review the history of his life, to know his worth and learn to value his example and his services. Let us, with a solemn pleasure, visit his tomb; there to drop a tear of affection, and heave a fervent sigh, over departed greatness. . . . There let us pluck a sprig of the willow and the laurel that shade the ashes of a WASHINGTON, and bear it on our bosoms, to remind us of his amiable virtues, his distinguished achievements, and our irreparable loss!. . . . Then let us resume our stations in life, and animated by his illustrious example, cheerfully attend to the duties assigned us, of improving the advantages, secured to us by the toils of the revolution, and the acquisition of independence.

Charles S. Hyneman and Donald S. Lutz, eds., *American Political Writing During the Founding Era: 1760–1805*, vol. 2 (Indianapolis: Liberty Fund, 1983).

Reader's Guide

1. We've all been faced with situations where we can choose to tell the truth or we can choose to lie. How have those lies affected your life negatively? In what ways can telling the truth make your life easier?

2. Do you think not telling the truth has a greater effect on you or on the other person?

3. Think about a time when you knew you were

---

being lied to. How did this make you feel? Did this have any effect on your feelings toward the other person? Explain your answer.

4. Is there a specific lie you've told in the past that has had a major impact on your life? What actions can you take to avoid lying in the future?

5. Some people like to measure their lies by how big or small they are. For instance, a white lie is considered to be a small lie that is supposedly harmless, or even beneficial, in the long term. Do you think it's ever okay to tell a lie? Explain your answer.

6. All lies have an impact on your life, your relationships, and the rest of the world. Do you

think the size of a lie determines how much of an impact it will have? Why or why not?

7. Should lying be acceptable when it is intended to protect someone else? Why or why not?

8. Why do you think it's easier to lie than to tell the truth in certain situations? Make a list of some situations you've been in where lying was an easier option than telling the truth. Explain why it was easier.

9. Think of the first lie you can remember telling. What do you think motivated you to not tell the truth?

10. Do you think learning about "the events

and decisions that have shaped the lives and nations of those who have gone before us" affects the way you interact with the world?

11. Sometime during Andy's study of the Dark Ages and Middle Ages, he uncovered an odd paradox: *the past* is what is real and true, while *history* is merely what someone recorded. Explain what this means to you.

12. Andy states, "Very few of us intentionally connect the truth of the past with the realities of where we have ended up today." How important is the truth, and what effect does it have on our future? Why do you think we have a difficult time connecting the truth of the past with the realities of where we have ended up today?

13. Why do you think the eleven million people sent to Nazi concentration camps believed Hitler and were willing to go? Do you think people's level of power has an effect on how easy they are to believe?

14. Hitler said, "Make the lie big, make it simple, keep saying it, and eventually they will believe it." Why is a simple and big lie easier to believe than one that is small and detailed?

15. Andy asks a big question: "Does anyone believe that telling the truth will solve all a nation's problems?" What do you believe?

16. How do you answer this question: "Is lying to get elected acceptable? Even if the candidate's

intention is to get elected in order to do good works?"

17. What does it mean to "judge the 'bad guys' by their actions and the 'good guys' by their intentions"? Which matters more: your actions or your intentions?

Resources

After reading this book, you may be interested in taking steps toward becoming more involved in your country's direction. The Internet is a wonderful tool for accomplishing this. You can find out how to do any number of things such as contacting your congressional representative, registering to vote, learning more about your state's and city's elected officials, learning when your city council meets, and more, all by doing a simple Internet search.

I also encourage you to seek wisdom at your local library and bookstore. Add others' knowledge and experience to your own. Of course, you need to be diligent in this pursuit and make sure your sources are reputable. You cannot believe everything you hear. Take time, compare, and consider what you are hearing and reading.

Most importantly, never stop looking for the truth. As long as we have our sights set on the truth, we are moving in the right direction.

Notes

1. Plato, quoted in Ralph Waldo Emerson, "Eloquence," *Society and Solitude* (Boston: James R. Osgood & Co., 1870), 56.
2. Rudolph J. Rummel, *Democide: Nazi Genocide and Mass Murder* (New Brunswick, NJ: Transaction, 1992), 85–86.
3. Ibid.
4. Ibid., 14.
5. Rudolph J. Rummel, *Statistics of Democide* (New Brunswick, NJ: Transaction, 1992), 48.
6. Rudolph J. Rummel, *Lethal Politics: Soviet Genocide and Mass Murder Since 1917* (Piscataway, NJ: Transaction Publishers, 1990), 16.
7. Rummel, *Statistics of Democide*, 78.
8. Ibid., 178.
9. Ibid., 187.
10. Ibid., 153.
11. Ibid., 164–77.
12. Neal Bascomb, *Hunting Eichmann* (New York: Houghton Mifflin Harcourt, 2009), 6.
13. www.enotes.com/topic/List_of_Nazi_Concentration_camps.
14. Jewish Virtual Library, http://www.jewishvirtuallibrary.org/jsource/Holocaust/cclist.html.

15. http://brainyquote.com/quotes/authors/a/adolf_hitler_2
    .html.
16. Adolf Hitler, *Mein Kampf*, trans. James Murphy (New
    York: Mariner, 1998).
17. www.mongabay.com/history/germany/germany-historical
    _background_population.html.
18. http://wn.com/nsdap?orderby=published.
19. Erwin W. Lutzer, *When a Nation Forgets God* (Chicago:
    Moody, 2010), 22.
20. US Census Bureau, US & World Population Clocks,
    http://www.census.gov/popclock.
21. Andy Andrews, *The Heart Mender* (Nashville: Thomas
    Nelson, 2010), 141–42.
22. Andy Stanley, *The Principle of the Path: How to Get from
    Where You Are to Where You Want to Be* (Nashville:
    Thomas Nelson, 2009), 14.
23. Andy Andrews, *The Traveler's Summit* (Nashville: Thomas
    Nelson, 2011).
24. George Santayana, *The Life of Reason, or: The Phases of
    Human Progress*, vol. 1 (New York: Charles Scribner's
    Sons, 1905), 284.
25. James Garfield, "A Century of Congress," *Atlantic*, July
    1877, 63, 64.
26. Andrews, *The Traveler's Summit*, 176.

Bibliography

Andrews, Andy. *The Heart Mender*. Nashville: Thomas Nelson, 2010.

Andrews, Andy. *The Traveler's Summit*. Nashville: Thomas Nelson, 2011.

Bascomb, Neal. *Hunting Eichmann*. New York: Houghton Mifflin Harcourt, 2009.

Hitler, Adolf. *Mein Kampf* (James Murphy Translation). New York: Mariner, 1998.

Lutzer, Erwin W. *When a Nation Forgets God*. Chicago: Moody, 2010.

Reese, Charley. "The Five Hundred and Forty Five People Responsible for America's Woes." www.informationclearinghouse.info.

Rummel, Rudolph J. *Lethal Politics: Soviet Genocide*

and Mass Murder Since 1917. Piscataway, NJ:
Transaction Publishers, 1990.

Stanley, Andy. *The Principle of the Path: How to Get from Where You Are to Where You Want to Be.* Nashville: Thomas Nelson, 2009.

www.census.gov

www.historyplace.com

www.jewishvirtuallibrary.org

www.nuremberg.law.harvard.edu

www.Spartacus.schoolnet.co.uk

About the Author

Hailed by a *New York Times* reporter as "someone who has quietly become one of the most influential people in America," Andy Andrews is a bestselling novelist, speaker, and consultant for some of the world's most successful teams, largest corporations, and fastest-growing organizations. Listeners in almost one hundred countries have subscribed to his weekly podcast, *The Professional Noticer,* on AndyAndrews.com/podcast and other sites that offer podcast subscriptions.

Andy is also the creator of WisdomHarbour .com—a portal that is fast becoming one of the most shared websites of the decade. He has spoken at the request of four United States presidents and works closely with America's Special Operations Command.

Zig Ziglar said, "Andy Andrews is the best speaker I have ever seen."

Andy is the author of the *New York Times* bestsellers *The Noticer* and the modern classic *The Traveler's Gift*—which has sold millions of copies worldwide.

He lives in Orange Beach, Alabama, with his wife, Polly, and their two sons.

ATTENTION EDUCATORS!

FREE curriculum and resources have been created for you and your students!

THESE RESOURCES HAVE BEEN USED
IN MORE THAN 2500 SCHOOL SYSTEMS

Find a guide for your favorite book at
AndyAndrews.com/Education

ANDY ANDREWS PRESENTS

WISDOM HARBOUR

At Wisdom Harbour, your docking privileges are unlimited and with so many different moorings available, there is always room to pull in and tie up.

Check out all of our docks including...
Videos, Audiobooks, Interviews, Live Q & A, Exclusive Blogs, and Much More!

For more information, visit WisdomHarbour.com

The PROFESSIONAL
NOTICER

*Observations and Answers
with Andy Andrews*

AVAILABLE WHEREVER YOU
LISTEN TO YOUR PODCASTS.

IF YOU HAVE A QUESTION YOU WOULD LIKE ANDY TO ANSWER ON
THE PROFESSIONAL NOTICER, PLEASE CONTACT US AT:

1-800-726-ANDY
THEPROFESSIONALNOTICER@ANDYANDREWS.COM

ISBN: 978-0-7180-7732-7

THE LITTLE THINGS

WHY YOU REALLY SHOULD SWEAT THE SMALL STUFF

Have you ever wondered why we spend so much time and energy
thinking about the big challenges in our lives when all the evidence
proves it's actually the little things that change everything?
That's right...Absolutely everything.

THE NOTICER RETURNS

SOMETIMES YOU FIND PERSPECTIVE, AND SOMETIMES PERSPECTIVE FINDS YOU

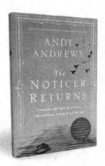

ISBN: 970-0-7852-3145-5

"Parents, coaches, employers, and employees...
Drop what you're doing and read this book!"

KURT WARNER
SUPER BOWL CHAMPION QUARTERBACK AND NFL BROADCASTER